Intermediate Latin Reader
Friends in Carthage

Rowan X. Adler

Rowan X. Adler

Copyright 2024

www.discoverlatin.com

Introduction

Welcome to *Friends in Carthage*! This book is designed to immerse you in the vibrant world of Roman Carthage while helping you build your Latin skills. Whether you are progressing from a beginner level or returning to Latin after some time, this book is an engaging resource that will support your journey.

The book is written in simplified Latin tailored to intermediate learners. Each chapter introduces common vocabulary and grammatical structures to deepen your understanding of the language. Through lively conversations and entertaining scenarios, you will explore friendships, challenges, and adventures set in a Roman context.

To get the most out of this book, we recommend the following strategies:

- Read actively: Don't rush through the text. Pause to look up unfamiliar words and review the grammar points covered in the chapter.

- Reread often: The repetitive nature of rereading helps reinforce vocabulary and sentence structures. Each reading will feel easier than the last.

- Practice speaking aloud: Latin comes alive when spoken. Try reading the dialogues aloud to improve your pronunciation and internalize the language.

- Use the notes and vocabulary: At the end of each chapter, you'll find helpful glossaries and explanations. These tools will guide you and clarify any difficult passages.

- Embrace the cultural context: The book doesn't just teach Latin—it also provides insights into Roman culture. Take a moment to appreciate the historical details woven into the story.

Remember, learning a language is a gradual process. Celebrate small victories along the way, like recognizing a new word or understanding a full sentence without translation. Over time, your confidence will grow, and Latin will feel less like a puzzle and more like a familiar friend.

Enjoy your journey with *Friends in Carthage*, and may you find both learning and joy in its pages!

Incolae Insulae et Discordiae

In angusta insula Carthaginiensi, anno Domini centesimo, quinque amici vitam modestam agebant. Severus, Rufus, Marcus, Aurelia, et Tullia in duobus cubiculi angustiis plenis habitabant. Puellae unum conclave habebant, iuvenes alterum. Parietes tenues omnem sonum transmittunt, ita ut clamores et rixae nullo modo celari possent. Paupertas eos coniungebat, sed saepe etiam discordiam alebat.

Erat vespera. Amici in cubiculo conglobati erant post diurnas occupationes. Marcus ad mensam sedebat et, scyphum vini tenens, ridebat. Rufus iuxta eum iacebat, dentes frendens. Severus in angulo libros suos inspiciebat, vultu serio. Aurelia crines suos ante speculum pectebat, dum Tullia, paene invisibilis et tacita, in obscuro angulo sedebat.

Subito Rufus, vultu suffuso, clamavit: "Quousque, Aurelia, Severum ita spectabis, quasi alius nemo hic adsit?"

Aurelia, vultu simul fastidioso et laeto, speculum deponens respondit: "Quid ad rem pertinet, Rufe? Severus saltem sapiens est et tacitus. Tu autem semper loqueris, sed nihil dicis."

Marcus, iam paululum ebrius, subridebat et dixit: "Audisne, Rufe? Tu stultior es cane tuo! Aurelia Severum amat, et nos reliquos contemnit."

Rufus ad Marcum versus, vultu iracundo, exclamavit: "Non loquere de canibus, Marce, cum tu ipse multo peior cane sis! Et Aurelia numquam te spectavit—illam ego certe amovebo!"

Aurelia interpellavit, oculis fulgentibus: "Vos ambo deliratis! Num ego umquam dixi me vobis favere?"

Severus, qui per totum tumultum librum tenebat, nunc lente surrexit et dixit: "Rufe, Marce, quiescite! Nonne sufficit quod in angusto conclavi habitamus? Cur vocibus vestris turbatis vitam nostram etiam peius redditis?"

Marcus, ridens, librum Severi manu rapuit. "O sapientissime Severe, num te paenitet quod Aurelia te amat?"

The Residents of the Apartment Building and Their Quarrels

In a cramped apartment building in Carthage, in the year 100 AD, five friends lived a modest life. Severus, Rufus, Marcus, Aurelia, and Tullia lived in two overcrowded rooms. The girls had one room, and the young men had another. The thin walls transmitted every sound, so that shouting and quarrels could by no means be hidden. Poverty united them, but often also fostered discord.

It was evening. The friends were gathered in their room after their daily tasks. Marcus sat at the table, holding a cup of wine and laughing. Rufus lay nearby, grinding his teeth. Severus was in a corner, examining his books with a serious expression. Aurelia was combing her hair in front of a mirror, while Tullia, almost invisible and silent, sat in a dark corner.

Suddenly, Rufus, his face flushed, shouted, "How long, Aurelia, will you look at Severus as if no one else is here?"

Aurelia, her face both disdainful and cheerful, put down the mirror and replied, "What does it matter, Rufus? At least Severus is wise and quiet. You, however, are always talking but say nothing."

Marcus, already a little drunk, smirked and said, "Do you hear that, Rufus? You are stupider than your dog! Aurelia loves Severus and despises the rest of us."

Rufus, turning to Marcus with an angry expression, exclaimed, "Don't speak of dogs, Marcus, when you yourself are far worse than one! And Aurelia has never looked at you—I will certainly take her away!"

Aurelia interrupted, her eyes flashing: "You are both insane! Did I ever say I favor either of you?"

Severus, who had been holding his book throughout the commotion, now slowly stood up and said, "Rufus, Marcus, be quiet! Isn't it bad enough that we live in this cramped room? Why do you make our lives even worse with your loud disputes?"

Marcus, laughing, snatched Severus' book from his hand. "Oh, most wise Severus, are you perhaps regretting that Aurelia loves you?"

Severus, vultu imperturbato, librum suum recipere conatus est. "Da mihi librum, Marce. Et te melius contine, antequam res peior fiat."

Aurelia, crines suos in cincinnos colligens, iterum verba fecit. "Vos omnes ridiculi estis! Nec Rufus nec Marcus mihi placet. Severus autem..." Ea subito tacuit, quasi nimium dixisset.

Rufus, hoc audiens, iratus exclamavit: "Ecce! Confessa est! Severum amat!"

Marcus e sella prosiliens clamavit: "Immo non! Aurelia mentitur! Me amat, non Severum!"

Tullia tandem, quae usque ad hoc tempus tacebat, magna voce clamavit: "Num ego hic ne sum quidem? Semper de Aurelia agitis, quasi ego nihil sim!"

Aurelia, oculis iridis plenis, se ad Tulliam convertit. "Tullia, non nunc! Non vides quantas stultitias isti loquuntur?"

Tullia tamen, indignata, perrexit: "Cur nemo mihi favet? Cur semper tu es in medio omnium sermonum, Aurelia?"

Tum clamor tam magnus factus est ut vicini e conclavibus suis voces emitterent. "Tacete!" unus per parietem clamavit. "Nonne scitis noctem esse?"

Sed intra cubiculum nullus siluit. Rufus manum suam in Marcum extendit, quasi eum pulsare vellet. Marcus, cavillans, dixit: "Non audeas, Rufe! Ego te uno ictu prosternam."

Severus inter eos stetit et magna voce clamavit: "Satis est! Ne quisquam manus moveat! Malum iam nimium fecistis."

Aurelia, iam irata, clamavit: "Vox vestra me exasperat! Num nihil aliud facere potestis nisi rixari?"

Rufus tamen, Aureliam spectans, dixit: "Cur tibi Severus tantum placet, Aurelia? Num non vides me meliorem esse?"

Aurelia manus ad caelum levavit et exclamavit: "Mehercule! Vos omnes insani estis!" Tum e cubiculo egressa est, ianuam magna vi claudens.

Severus, with an unperturbed expression, tried to take his book back. "Give me the book, Marcus. And control yourself better before things get worse."

Aurelia, gathering her hair into curls, spoke again. "You are all ridiculous! I like neither Rufus nor Marcus. Severus, however..." She suddenly fell silent, as if she had said too much.

Rufus, hearing this, shouted angrily: "Look! She has confessed! She loves Severus!"

Marcus jumped up from his chair and shouted: "Not true! Aurelia is lying! She loves me, not Severus!"

At last, Tullia, who had been silent until now, cried out loudly: "Am I even here? You always talk about Aurelia as if I don't exist!"

Aurelia, her eyes full of indignation, turned to Tullia. "Tullia, not now! Don't you see how foolishly they are speaking?"

Tullia, however, continued indignantly: "Why does no one care about me? Why are you always the center of every conversation, Aurelia?"

Then the shouting became so loud that the neighbors in the adjoining apartments raised their voices. "Be quiet!" one of them shouted through the wall. "Don't you know it's nighttime?"

But inside the room, no one quieted down. Rufus extended his hand toward Marcus, as if to strike him. Marcus, mocking, said: "Don't you dare, Rufus! I'll knock you down with one punch."

Severus stood between them and shouted loudly: "Enough! No one is to lay a hand on anyone else! You've already caused enough trouble."

Aurelia, now angry, shouted: "Your voices are driving me mad! Can't you do anything else but quarrel?"

Rufus, however, looking at Aurelia, said: "Why do you like Severus so much, Aurelia? Don't you see that I'm better?"

Aurelia raised her hands to the heavens and exclaimed: "By Hercules! You're all insane!" Then she left the room, slamming the door forcefully behind her.

Post discessum Aureliae, omnes per momentum tacuerunt. Marcus, risu simul acerbo et nervoso, dixit: "Haec tua culpa est, Rufe."

Rufus respondit: "Immo tua culpa! Si tu tacuisses, Aurelia mansisset."

Severus in sella resedit, vultu gravis. "Utinam vos ambo aliquando sapientiores fieretis. Aurelia abiit propter stultitiam vestram."

Tullia, quae lacrimas retinere conabatur, submurmuravit: "Semper Aurelia… Semper Aurelia. Num ego sum nihil?"

Iterum vicini per parietem clamaverunt: "Si non silueritis, vigilibus vos tradam!"

Severus suspiravit et, gravis voce, dixit: "Tacete, omnes. Iam satis turbae fecimus. Aureliam quaerere debemus, priusquam aliquid peius fiat."

Marcus humeros sustulit. "Si vult abire, quid ad nos?"

Rufus tamen surrexit et dixit: "Non licet illam solam relinquere. Ego eam quaesiturus sum."

Severus eum retinuit manu. "Ne insipienter age, Rufe. Mane hic, et maneamus tranquilli."

Silentium cubiculum implevit. Rufus tamen prope ianuam stabat, Marcus iterum vino se consolabatur, et Severus in cogitationibus haerebat. Tullia in angulo mansit, sola, et conspectum Aureliae, quae irata discesserat, mente volvebat.

After Aurelia's departure, everyone fell silent for a moment. Marcus, with a bitter and nervous laugh, said: "This is your fault, Rufus."

Rufus replied: "No, it's your fault! If you had kept quiet, Aurelia would have stayed."

Severus sat back down in his chair with a serious expression. "If only you two would grow wiser someday. Aurelia left because of your foolishness."

Tullia, trying to hold back tears, murmured: "Always Aurelia... Always Aurelia. Am I nothing?"

Again, the neighbors shouted through the wall: "If you don't quiet down, I'll call the watchmen on you!"

Severus sighed and said in a grave voice: "Be silent, all of you. We've caused enough commotion. We must look for Aurelia before something worse happens."

Marcus shrugged. "If she wants to leave, what does it matter to us?"

Rufus, however, stood up and said: "We cannot leave her alone. I'm going to find her."

Severus held him back with his hand. "Don't act rashly, Rufus. Stay here, and let's remain calm."

Silence filled the room. Rufus, however, stood near the door. Marcus once again consoled himself with wine, while Severus was lost in thought. Tullia remained in the corner, alone, replaying in her mind the image of Aurelia storming out in anger.

Cursus Post Aureliam

Post tumultum nocturnum, Severus, Rufus, Marcus, et Tullia in cubiculo sedebant, vultibus anxiis. Aurelia nondum redierat, et vicini iam minati erant vigilibus. Severus, vultu gravi, tandem silentium rupit.

"Non possumus hic sedere et nihil agere," inquit. "Aurelia sola foris est. Nec locus nec hora sunt tuti."

"Tuus est error, Rufe," Marcus respondit, iam rubore suffusus. "Si non tam stulte egisses, Aurelia mansisset."

"Stulte egissem?" Rufus indignatus exclamavit. "Immo tu illam semper provocas! Ego certe eam inveniam!"

"Desinite, ambo," Severus ait, manum tollens. "Si rixamini, nihil agemus. Eamus omnes."

Tullia, quae in angulo tacita sederat, tandem verba fecit. "Certe debemus eam invenire," inquit mordaciter, "sed scilicet Aurelia iterum erit in centro omnium rerum, et ego nihil."

Severus eam aspexit, sed nihil dixit. Mox omnes conclave reliquerunt et in viam processerunt. In vicinia insulae obscura, voces mercatorum et latratus canum audiebantur.

"Dividamus," Severus proposuit. "Marcus et Rufus, vos ad sinistram quaerite. Tullia et ego ad dextram ibimus."

Rufus murmuravit sed consensit. "Si Aureliam inveniam," inquit, "ego primus loquar!"

Marcus risit. "Si eam invenias, prius tibi ignoscere debet quod tam ineptus es."

"Tacete et ite," Severus cum exasperatione dixit. Duo iuvenes discesserunt, relicto Severo cum Tullia.

"Numquam cessant," Tullia suspiravit. "Quid putas, Severe? Num Aurelia vere te amat?"

"De hoc nunc non loquar," Severus respondit, oculos in viam figens. "Curae nobis est eam invenire, non quid sentiatur."

The Search for Aurelia

After the commotion of the night, Severus, Rufus, Marcus, and Tullia sat in the room, their faces anxious. Aurelia still had not returned, and the neighbors were already threatening to call the watchmen. Severus, with a serious expression, finally broke the silence.

"We cannot just sit here and do nothing," he said. "Aurelia is out alone. Neither the place nor the hour is safe."

"This is your fault, Rufus," Marcus replied, his face already flushed. "If you hadn't acted so foolishly, Aurelia would have stayed."

"Acted foolishly?" Rufus exclaimed indignantly. "It's you who always provoke her! I will certainly find her!"

"Stop it, both of you," Severus said, raising his hand. "If you keep arguing, we'll accomplish nothing. Let's all go."

Tullia, who had been sitting quietly in the corner, finally spoke. "Of course we must find her," she said bitterly, "but of course Aurelia will once again be at the center of everything, and I will be nothing."

Severus looked at her but said nothing. Soon, they all left the room and went out into the street. In the dark neighborhood around the apartment building, the voices of merchants and the barking of dogs could be heard.

"Let's split up," Severus suggested. "Marcus and Rufus, you search to the left. Tullia and I will go to the right."

Rufus muttered but agreed. "If I find Aurelia," he said, "I will be the first to speak with her!"

Marcus laughed. "If you find her, she'll have to forgive you first for being so clumsy."

"Be quiet and go," Severus said with exasperation. The two young men left, leaving Severus with Tullia.

"They never stop," Tullia sighed. "What do you think, Severus? Does Aurelia really love you?"

"I won't talk about that now," Severus replied, fixing his eyes on the road ahead. "Our concern is to find her, not to talk about feelings."

Dum haec loquebantur, Rufus et Marcus in altero angulo insulae ambulabant. Rufus ianuam pulsavit. "Aurelia, esne hic?" vocavit.

Ianua aperta est, sed non Aurelia apparuit. Vetula irata eos spectavit. "Quid vultis?" clamavit. "Cur me perturbatis?"

"Quaerimus amicam nostram," Marcus cito respondit. "Nonne vidisti puellam crinibus flavis?"

Vetula oculos arcte coartavit. "Nulla hic est. Discedite, antequam virga mea vos tangat!"

Marcus et Rufus, risu vix retento, celeriter discesserunt. Dum in altera domo pulsant, piscator philosophus e fenestra caput ostendit. "Quos quaeritis, iuvenes?" rogavit.

"Amicam nostram, Aureliam," Rufus respondit. "Quid nobis consulis?"

"Amicitia saepe, sicut pisces, captu difficilis est," philosophus graviter respondit. "Sed quaerite, et forsitan invenietis."

"Euge, magna utilitas!" Marcus risit. "Melius pisces venderet quam sapientiam."

Interea, Severus et Tullia ad campum forensem pervenerunt. Pueri ludentes eos circumvenerunt et clamaverunt: "Nummi! Da nobis nummos, et dicemus quid scimus!"

Severus suspiravit et unum nummum ex sacculo protulit. "Vidistisne puellam crinibus flavis?" rogavit.

"Vidimus!" unus ex pueris clamavit. "Currebat versus tabernam vini!"

Severus et Tullia ad tabernam cucurrerunt, ubi Rufus et Marcus iam convenerant. Taberna plena erat clamorum, odoris vini, et strepitus. Aurelia tamen nusquam videbatur.

"Num alii viderunt eam?" Rufus rogavit tabernarium.

"Puellae hic saepe veniunt," respondit tabernarius subridens. "Quid vultis bibere?"

While this was happening, Rufus and Marcus were walking in another part of the apartment building. Rufus knocked on a door. "Aurelia, are you here?" he called.

The door opened, but it was not Aurelia who appeared. An angry old woman glared at them. "What do you want?" she shouted. "Why are you disturbing me?"

"We're looking for our friend," Marcus quickly replied. "Haven't you seen a girl with blonde hair?"

The old woman narrowed her eyes sharply. "There's no one here. Go away, before my stick finds you!"

Marcus and Rufus, barely able to hold back their laughter, quickly left. As they knocked on another door, a fisherman philosopher stuck his head out of a window. "Who are you looking for, young men?" he asked.

"Our friend, Aurelia," Rufus replied. "What do you advise us?"

"Friendship, like fish, is often hard to catch," the philosopher replied gravely. "But keep looking, and perhaps you'll find her."

"Wonderful, such great advice!" Marcus laughed. "He'd do better to sell fish than wisdom."

Meanwhile, Severus and Tullia arrived at the town square. A group of children playing there surrounded them and shouted: "Coins! Give us coins, and we'll tell you what we know!"

Severus sighed and pulled a coin from his purse. "Have you seen a girl with blonde hair?" he asked.

"We have!" one of the children shouted. "She was running toward the wine shop!"

Severus and Tullia ran to the wine shop, where Rufus and Marcus had already gathered. The shop was full of noise, the smell of wine, and general commotion. However, Aurelia was nowhere to be seen.

"Did anyone else see her?" Rufus asked the shopkeeper.

"Girls often come here," the shopkeeper replied with a smirk. "What do you want to drink?"

"Minime," Severus interpellavit. "Nos puellam quaerimus, non vinum."

Marcus tamen iam scyphum vini rapuerat. "Haec rixa sit vana nisi aliquid ex hoc capiamus," dixit ridens. "Euge! Salutem meam bibamus."

Dum Severus Rufum dissuadere conatur, Tullia in angulo cum tabernario loquebatur. "Scisne," susurravit, "te oculis pulchris esse?"

Tabernarius tamen abrupto risu respondit: "Si pecuniam tuam solves, oculi mei etiam pulchriores erunt."

"Audacissime!" Tullia exclamavit, rubore suffusa, et discessit.

Post multa tumultuosa momenta, quidam in taberna clamavit: "Puella crinibus flavis currit versus forum!"

Omnes celeriter exierunt. In foro viderunt mulierem vestitu rubro quae Aurelia esse videbatur. Rufus ad eam cucurrit et bracchium eius cepit.

"Aurelia, invenimus te!" exclamavit.

Mulier irata se convertit. "Quid audes, iuvenis?" clamavit. "Sum uxor gladiatoris!"

Marcus, qui post Rufum stabat, risit. "Rufe, gladiatores non irasci voles."

Mulier tamen vocem auxilium clamavit, et omnes amici celeriter effugerunt, inter risum et pavorem.

Tandem Aurelia ipsa apparuit, vultu sereno. "Quid vultis, insani?" rogavit. "Numquam periculum fuit. In balneis eram."

"Balneis?" Rufus clamavit. "Totum diem te quaerimus!"

"Si minus rixati essetis," Aurelia respondit, "fortasse melius tempus haberetis."

Cum amici domum redirent, piscator philosophus iterum in gradibus sedebat. "Amicitia saepe, sicut pisces," dixit, "tandem capitur, si satis patientiam habetis."

"Nothing," Severus interrupted. "We're looking for a girl, not wine."

Marcus, however, had already snatched a cup of wine. "This argument would be pointless unless we gain something from it," he said, laughing. "Cheers! Let's drink to my health."

While Severus was trying to dissuade Rufus, Tullia was talking to the shopkeeper in a corner. "Did you know," she whispered, "that you have beautiful eyes?"

The shopkeeper, however, burst into abrupt laughter and replied: "If you pay your bill, my eyes will become even more beautiful."

"How dare you!" Tullia exclaimed, blushing deeply, and walked away.

After several chaotic moments, someone in the tavern shouted: "A girl with blonde hair is running toward the forum!"

They all rushed out. In the forum, they saw a woman in a red dress who looked like Aurelia. Rufus ran up to her and grabbed her arm.

"Aurelia, we've found you!" he exclaimed.

The angry woman turned around. "How dare you, young man?" she shouted. "I am the wife of a gladiator!"

Marcus, who was standing behind Rufus, laughed. "Rufus, you don't want to anger gladiators."

The woman, however, cried out for help, and all the friends quickly fled, half laughing and half terrified.

At last, Aurelia herself appeared, her expression calm. "What do you want, you lunatics?" she asked. "There was never any danger. I was at the baths."

"The baths?" Rufus shouted. "We've been searching for you all day!"

"If you had argued less," Aurelia replied, "perhaps you would have had a better time."

As the friends returned home, the fisherman philosopher was once again sitting on the steps. "Friendship, like fish," he said, "is finally caught if you have enough patience."

"Non iterum!" Marcus murmuravit. Aurelia autem risit et eos omnes ad insulam duxit. "Utinam diem melius incepissetis," dixit, "sed finem bonum habet."

"Not again!" Marcus muttered. But Aurelia laughed and led them all back to the apartment. "I wish you had started the day better," she said, "but it has ended well."

Discordia Domestica

Tullia sola in cubiculo sedebat, querimoniis solitis afflicta. "Semper Aurelia!" sibi dixit, vultu tristi. "Num ego sum statua? Num ego non sum pulchra?" Dum haec murmurabat, ianua leniter pulsa est. Tullia surrexit et dubitanter aperuit. Severus ante limen stabat, vultu placido sed oculis micantibus.

"Salve, Tullia," Severus ait, introrsus gradum faciens. "Putavi te solam esse. Possumne intrare?"

"Cur non?" Tullia respondit, leviter rubens. "Quid vis, Severe?"

Severus in sella prope fenestram sedens dixit: "Multa cogitabam, Tullia. Soleo te videre, sed numquam satis tecum loquor. Mihi videris... diversa."

"Diversa?" Tullia mirata inquit, sed intus iam laetitia ardebat. "Quomodo diversa?"

"Non sicut Aurelia," Severus respondit. "Quae semper loquitur, semper clamat. Tu autem... grata es, tranquilla, elegans."

Tullia in angulo sedens vultum avertit, ne Severus ruborem eius videret. "Saepe nemo me observat," dixit leniter. "Omnes Aureliam spectant."

Severus paulum propior factus est. "Sed ego te video, Tullia," susurravit. "Tu digna es admiratione."

Dum haec loquebantur, Aurelia, quae paulo ante redierat, extra ianuam stetit. Primo curiosa, verba Severi audita repente irata facta est. "Ego... diversa? Semper clamo?" sibi dixit submurmurans. "Videamus quid hic agatur!"

Aurelia ianuam repentina vi aperuit. "Severe!" clamavit. "Quid hic agis cum Tullia?"

Tullia e sella exsiluit. "Cur tu semper nos perturbas, Aurelia? Non potes aliquando tacere?"

"Tacere? Ego sum quae tacere debeat?" Aurelia irata respondit. "Tu autem, perfida! Num Severum mihi auferre conaris?"

Domestic Discord

Tullia was sitting alone in the room, distressed by her usual complaints. "Always Aurelia!" she said to herself, her face sad. "Am I just a statue? Am I not beautiful?" While she was murmuring these things, the door was gently knocked. Tullia got up and hesitantly opened it. Severus stood at the threshold, his expression calm but his eyes gleaming.

"Hello, Tullia," Severus said, stepping inside. "I thought you were alone. May I come in?"

"Why not?" Tullia replied, blushing slightly. "What do you want, Severus?"

Sitting in a chair near the window, Severus said: "I've been thinking a lot, Tullia. I often see you, but I never speak with you enough. You seem to me... different."

"Different?" Tullia asked in surprise, though inside she was already glowing with joy. "How am I different?"

"Not like Aurelia," Severus replied. "She always talks, always shouts. But you... you are kind, calm, elegant."

Tullia, sitting in a corner, turned her face away so that Severus would not see her blush. "No one often notices me," she said softly. "Everyone looks at Aurelia."

Severus moved a little closer. "But I see you, Tullia," he whispered. "You are worthy of admiration."

While they were speaking, Aurelia, who had returned a short time earlier, stood outside the door. At first curious, she suddenly became angry when she heard Severus's words. "I... different? Always shouting?" she muttered to herself. "Let's see what's going on here!"

Aurelia flung the door open with sudden force. "Severus!" she shouted. "What are you doing here with Tullia?"

Tullia jumped up from her chair. "Why do you always disturb us, Aurelia? Can't you ever be quiet?"

"Be quiet? I'm the one who should be quiet?" Aurelia replied angrily. "And you, traitor! Are you trying to steal Severus from me?"

"Severus non est tuus!" Tullia exclamavit, manus in latera ponens. "Num tu omnes viros possidere vis?"

Interim Severus, qui clamores crescere viderat, surrexit et retro cessit. "Puellae, placate vos," dixit, sed voces feminarum eum paene oppresserunt. Subito Severus, occasione captata, per ianuam effugit.

Aurelia, ubi eum abisse animadvertit, clamavit: "Tullia! Tu eum fugasti!"

"Non ego!" Tullia respondit. "Tu es quae semper rixas facis!"

Verba in manus transierunt. Aurelia crines Tulliae cepit, Tullia autem aurem Aureliae vellicavit. Clamoribus eorum vicini iam advigilaverant. Pugna in pavimentum devoluta est, ubi Tullia capillos Aureliae traxit, Aurelia autem sandalia sua ad Tulliam iactavit.

Rufus et Marcus hoc tempore domum redierunt, clamores audientes. Rufus ianuam aperuit et subito substitit. "O di immortales!" exclamavit. "Quid hic fit? Gladiatores sunt?"

Marcus, risu suffocatus, in medium cubiculum cucurrit. "Desinite, puellae!" clamavit. "Num tam turpe est ut Severus vos relinquat?"

Aurelia et Tullia, anhelantes et crinibus inordinatis, tandem cessaverunt. "Severus," Aurelia dixit, "ubi est?"

"Abiit," Marcus respondit, umeris sublatis. "Sed ne curetis. Nos hic sumus ad vos consolandas."

Rufus ad Aureliam accessit, vultu serio. "Num vis animum tuum levare?" rogavit. "Ego te semper admiratus sum."

Marcus Tulliam, quae adhuc spiritum colligebat, spectavit. "Tullia," ait molli voce, "num non melius est pacem servare? Ego te intellego."

Paulum silentium fuit, sed mox risus timidus ex ore Aureliae emanavit. "Forsitan Severus non valet tantum quantum putabamus," dixit.

"Severus is not yours!" Tullia exclaimed, placing her hands on her hips. "Do you want to possess every man?"

Meanwhile, Severus, seeing the shouting intensify, stood up and backed away. "Girls, calm down," he said, but their voices nearly drowned him out. Suddenly, seizing the opportunity, Severus slipped out through the door.

When Aurelia noticed he had gone, she shouted: "Tullia! You made him run away!"

"Not me!" Tullia replied. "You're the one who always starts fights!"

The argument escalated to physical blows. Aurelia grabbed Tullia's hair, but Tullia pinched Aurelia's ear. Their shouting had already awakened the neighbors. The fight spilled onto the floor, where Tullia pulled Aurelia's hair while Aurelia threw her sandals at Tullia.

At this moment, Rufus and Marcus returned home, hearing the commotion. Rufus opened the door and immediately froze. "By the immortal gods!" he exclaimed. "What's happening here? Are these gladiators?"

Marcus, choking with laughter, rushed into the middle of the room. "Stop it, girls!" he shouted. "Is it really so terrible that Severus left you?"

Aurelia and Tullia, panting and with their hair in disarray, finally stopped. "Severus," Aurelia said, "where is he?"

"He's gone," Marcus replied with a shrug. "But don't worry. We're here to console you."

Rufus approached Aurelia with a serious expression. "Would you like to lighten your mood?" he asked. "I've always admired you."

Marcus looked at Tullia, who was still catching her breath. "Tullia," he said softly, "isn't it better to keep the peace? I understand you."

There was a brief silence, but soon a timid laugh escaped from Aurelia. "Perhaps Severus isn't worth as much as we thought," she said.

"Recte dicis," Tullia adiecit, oculos demittens. "Vos tamen... non estis omnino mali."

"Non omnino mali?" Rufus risit. "Videbis, Aurelia."

Marcus Tulliam ad se leniter traxit. "Melius est ridere quam pugnare, nonne?"

Mox duo paria in angulis cubiculi sedebant, suaviter colloquentes. Marcus et Tullia de pueritia loquebantur, Rufus autem Aureliam de spe futura rogabat. Sol tandem occidit, et tranquillitas ad domum rediit.

"You're right," Tullia added, lowering her eyes. "You two, however... you're not entirely bad."

"Not entirely bad?" Rufus laughed. "You'll see, Aurelia."

Marcus gently pulled Tullia closer to him. "It's better to laugh than to fight, isn't it?"

Soon, the two pairs were sitting in opposite corners of the room, conversing softly. Marcus and Tullia talked about their childhoods, while Rufus asked Aurelia about her hopes for the future. At last, the sun set, and peace returned to the home.

Severus et Taberna

Noctu Severus, mente turbata post tumultus cum Aurelia et Tullia, tabernam in vicinia quaesivit. Luna plena inter nubes raris radiis lucebat, dum Severus, vultu gravi sed oculis vini cupientibus, per viam errabat. Mox tabernam invenit, unde cantus et strepitus resonabant.

Intravit et ad mensam in angulo consedit. Tabernarius, vir pinguis vultuque hilari, ad eum accessit. "Quid vis, iuvenis?" rogavit.

"Vinum," Severus respondit, graviter suspirans. "Cras de vita cogitabo, sed nunc bibo."

Tabernarius, subridens, amphoram vini posuit ante Severum. "Hoc vinum tibi animum levabit," ait. "Cave tamen, ne nimis bibas!"

Severus primum poculum celeriter hausit, deinde alterum. Dum vinum bibebat, cantus convivis crebrescebat. Vir quidam iuxta eum stans clavam levavit et clamavit: "Cantemus omnes de amore et fortuna!"

"De amore?" Severus respondit, iam vino audacior. "Amor me solum vexat! Ego cantabo de... tristitia!"

Convivae riserunt, et Severus in mensam ascendit, vinum poculo tenens. "Audite me!" clamavit. Tum canticum ridiculum coepit:

"Amor me vexat, vinum me iuvat,

Quid mihi opus est nisi amphora nova?"

Convivae plausus dederunt, clamantes: "Bene cantas, Severe! Iterum canamus!"

Interea lupa quaedam, mulier vestitu splendenti vultuque callido, tabernam intravit. Severum statim conspexit et ad eum accessit, leniter ridens. "Salve, pulchre iuvenis," susurravit. "Cur solus hic es?"

Severus, iam vino animatus, respondit: "Non solus sum. Vinum me comitatur!"

Severus and the Tavern

At night, Severus, his mind troubled after the quarrels with Aurelia and Tullia, wandered the neighborhood looking for a tavern. The full moon shone intermittently through the clouds as Severus, with a serious expression but eyes craving wine, roamed the street. Soon he found a tavern from which singing and noise echoed.

He entered and sat at a table in the corner. The tavern keeper, a fat man with a cheerful face, approached him. "What do you want, young man?" he asked.

"Wine," Severus replied with a heavy sigh. "I'll think about life tomorrow, but tonight I drink."

The tavern keeper, smiling, placed a pitcher of wine in front of Severus. "This wine will lift your spirits," he said. "But beware, don't drink too much!"

Severus quickly downed the first cup, then a second. As he drank the wine, the singing of the other patrons grew louder. A man standing nearby raised a club and shouted: "Let us all sing of love and fortune!"

"Love?" Severus replied, emboldened by the wine. "Love only torments me! I'll sing about... sadness!"

The patrons laughed, and Severus climbed onto the table, holding his cup of wine. "Listen to me!" he shouted. Then he began a ridiculous song:

"Love torments me, wine delights me, What do I need but another pitcher?"

The patrons applauded, shouting: "Well sung, Severus! Let's sing it again!"

Meanwhile, a harlot, a woman in splendid clothing with a cunning look—entered the tavern. She immediately spotted Severus and approached him, smiling softly. "Hello, handsome young man," she whispered. "Why are you here alone?"

Severus, now emboldened by the wine, replied: "I'm not alone. Wine is keeping me company!"

Lupa ad eum propius accessit et manum suam super brachium eius posuit. "Vinum bonum est," inquit, "sed melior ego sum. Nonne vis mecum venire? Noctem iucundam tibi dabo."

Severus risit. "Noli me vexare, mulier. Ego... ego sum philosophus, non stultus!"

Sed lupa non destitit. "Philosophus?" subridens dixit. "Tum philosophia tua te in gaudia ducere potest. Cur non experiris?"

Dum lupa paulatim ad sedem Severi se inclinabat, ianua tabernae subito aperta est. Soror Severi, Flavia, cum marito suo Iulio ingressa est. Ubi spectaculum vidit, lupa iam in genibus Severi inclinata, Flavia exclamavit: "Severe! Quid hic agis?"

Severus surrexit, sed vinum iam sensus eius turbaverat. "Flavia!" clamavit, paulum vacillans. "Quid agis hic? Ego... ego philosophiam discuto!"

"Philosophiam?" Flavia irata respondit, lupae manum a Severi brachio amovens. "Haec mulier philosophia tua est? Potius vinum te stultum fecit!"

Iulius, vir placidus sed severus, Severum spectavit. "Frater, non decet te sic in taberna invenire. Quid si vicini te viderent?"

Lupa, quae irata erat quod scaena turbata erat, in Iulium verba iecit: "Quis me culpat? Ego nihil mali facio!"

Flavia autem non tacebat. "Discede, lupa!" clamavit. "Fratrem meum nunc domum ducam!"

Severus, iam paene collapsus, murmuravit: "Non opus est... ego ipse domum... inveniam."

"Immo," Iulius respondit, "nos te ducemus. Tu ambulare ne potes quidem!"

Cum multa rixa et clamore, Flavia et Iulius Severum de taberna extraxerunt, dum convivae ridebant et cantabant:

"Severus amat vinum, sed lupa magis,

Soror autem fraternum caput pulsat saepe gratis!"

The harlot moved closer to Severus and placed her hand on his arm. "Wine is good," she said, "but I am better. Don't you want to come with me? I will give you a delightful night."

Severus laughed. "Don't bother me, woman. I... I am a philosopher, not a fool!"

But the harlot persisted. "A philosopher?" she said with a sly smile. "Then your philosophy should lead you to enjoy yourself. Why not give it a try?"

As the harlot leaned closer to Severus in his seat, the tavern door suddenly swung open. Severus's sister, Flavia, entered with her husband, Julius. When Flavia saw the scene, with the harlot already leaning on Severus's knees, she exclaimed: "Severus! What are you doing here?"

Severus stood up, but the wine had already muddled his senses. "Flavia!" he shouted, swaying slightly. "What are you doing here? I... I am discussing philosophy!"

"Philosophy?" Flavia replied angrily, pulling the harlot's hand off Severus's arm. "Is this woman your philosophy? It's the wine that has made you foolish!"

Julius, a calm but stern man, looked at Severus. "Brother, it's not proper to find you like this in a tavern. What if the neighbors saw you?"

The harlot, irritated that her scene had been disrupted, snapped at Julius: "Who's blaming me? I've done nothing wrong!"

Flavia, however, wasn't silent. "Get out of here, harlot!" she shouted. "I'm taking my brother home now!"

Severus, nearly collapsing, muttered: "There's no need... I can find my way... home myself."

"On the contrary," Julius replied, "we'll take you. You can barely walk!"

With much arguing and shouting, Flavia and Julius dragged Severus out of the tavern, while the patrons laughed and sang:

"Severus loves wine, but the harlot even more,
Yet his sister strikes his foolish head for free forevermore!"

Severus in via inter Flaviam et Lucium pendens murmurat: "Flavia, cur... cur semper me vexas?"

"Quia tu stultus es," Flavia respondit, sed leniter subridebat. "Ego autem te servare debeo."

Post longum iter, Flavia et Iulius Severum ad cubiculum eius reduxerunt. Cum eum in lecto posuissent, Flavia dixit: "Mane hic, Severe. Cras de vino et philosophia cogita."

Iulius adiecit: "Et, amabo te, noli iterum ad tabernam ire."

Severus, iam semisomnus, respondit: "Vinum... bonum est. Amor... melior."

Flavia caput movit et risit, Iulio manu data. "Vale, frater. Dormi et somnia de sapientia tua!"

Tandem, nocte tranquilla, domum reliquerunt, Severus autem in somnis cantavit:

"Amor me vexat, sed vinum me docet.

Soror me curat, ne lupa me ducat."

Severus, swaying between Flavia and Julius as they supported him, murmured: "Flavia, why... why do you always bother me?"

"Because you're foolish," Flavia replied, though she smiled gently. "But I have to take care of you."

After a long walk, Flavia and Julius brought Severus back to his room. Once they had laid him on his bed, Flavia said: "Stay here, Severus. Tomorrow, think about wine and philosophy."

Julius added: "And, please, don't go back to the tavern again."

Severus, already half-asleep, replied: "Wine... is good. Love... is better."

Flavia shook her head and laughed, taking Julius's hand. "Goodnight, brother. Sleep and dream of your wisdom!"

Finally, in the calm of the night, they left the house. Severus, however, sang in his sleep:

"Love torments me, but wine teaches me.

My sister saves me, lest the harlot lead me."

Amici et Ludi in Amphitheatro

Post multos dies rixarum et tumultuum, quinque amici—Severus, Rufus, Marcus, Aurelia, et Tullia—tandem pacem invenerant. Mane uno die, dum omnes in insula congregati erant, Marcus chartam manu tenens laetus advenit, vultu exsultante et oculis micantibus.

"Ludii in amphitheatro Carthaginis nuntiati sunt!" clamavit, chartam altius tollens. "Gladiatores, venationes, pugnae bestiarum—spectaculum mirabile! Nonne ire volumus?"

Aurelia statim exsultavit. "O di immortales! Gladiatores! Semper eos spectare volui. Quam laeta sum!"

"Et ego!" Tullia exclamavit, oculis iam ardentibus. "Gladiatores pugnant sicut dei! Quid aliud melius esse potest?"

Rufus, subridens et humeros tollens, respondit: "Vos puellae estis sanguinariae. Ego malim vinum bibere in umbra quam homines gladios vibrantes spectare."

"Tacete, Rufe," Aurelia minaci oculo dixit. "Amphitheatrum non solum de gladiatoribus est, sed de arte, de audacia. Num vere non intellegis?"

Severus, qui solito graviter sedebat, manum ad mentum posuit et lentus respondit: "Spectaculum bonum videtur, sed memento, Marce, pretium nobis omnibus solvere necesse erit."

"Non cures, Severe," Marcus risit, pectore inflato. "Hodie ego omnia solvam. Hic dies erit magnificus!"

Cum omnibus placuisset, amici consilium ceperunt. Dum per vias Carthaginis iter faciebant, turbae eos circumdabant. Homines festinantes ad amphitheatrum clamabant, venditores autem merces suas laudabant: "Panes recentes! Aqua frigida! Coronam tuam emite pro victore tuo!"

"Specta illas coronas aureas!" Tullia clamavit, digito monstrans ad tabernam. "Fortasse gladiatori pulcherrimo coronam offerre possumus."

Friends and Games in the Amphitheatre

After many days of quarrels and commotion, the five friends—Severus, Rufus, Marcus, Aurelia, and Tullia—finally found peace. One morning, while they were all gathered in the apartment building, Marcus arrived cheerfully holding a piece of parchment, his face glowing with excitement and his eyes sparkling.

"Games have been announced in the Carthage amphitheatre!" he exclaimed, raising the parchment high. "Gladiators, hunts, beast fights—a marvelous spectacle! Don't we want to go?"

Aurelia immediately burst with excitement. "Oh, immortal gods! Gladiators! I've always wanted to see them. How happy I am!"

"And I!" Tullia exclaimed, her eyes already alight. "Gladiators fight like gods! What could be better?"

Rufus, smiling and shrugging his shoulders, replied: "You girls are bloodthirsty. I'd rather drink wine in the shade than watch men swinging swords."

"Be quiet, Rufus," Aurelia said with a threatening look. "The amphitheatre isn't just about gladiators—it's about art, about courage. Don't you truly understand?"

Severus, who was sitting with his usual seriousness, placed a hand on his chin and slowly responded: "It sounds like a good spectacle, but remember, Marcus, we'll all need to pay the entrance fee."

"Don't worry, Severus," Marcus laughed, puffing out his chest. "Today I'll pay for everything. This day will be magnificent!"

Once everyone agreed, the friends made their plan. As they walked through the streets of Carthage, crowds surrounded them. People hurrying to the amphitheatre shouted, while vendors praised their goods: "Fresh bread! Cold water! Buy a wreath for your champion!"

"Look at those golden wreaths!" Tullia cried, pointing to a stall. "Perhaps we could offer a wreath to the most handsome gladiator!"

"Pulcherrimo?" Marcus mordaciter respondit. "Num pulchritudo eos adiuvat ut vivos maneant?"

"Non solum pulchritudo," Aurelia addidit, subridens. "Sed victoria et audacia. Gladiatores sunt viri fortes."

Cum turbas pertransissent, amici amphitheatrum ingens conspexerunt. Moles lapidea tam alta erat ut caput tollere necesse esset ad summitatem aspiciendam. Intus iam clamor spectatorum resonabat, quasi proelium iam coepisset.

Amici loca invenerunt in parte media, unde totum spectaculum bene spectari poterat. Aurelia et Tullia anticipatione ardebant, oculis in arenam fixis. Rufus et Marcus tamen reclinati manserunt, subridens et inter se susurrantes. Severus, vultu gravi, sedebat, tacitus.

Tuba subito sonuit, et omnes tacuerunt. Praeco in arenam processit et magna voce clamavit: "Cives Carthaginis! Ludii nunc incipiunt! Gladiatores et bestiae coram vobis certabunt. Spectate et gaudete!"

Portae magnae apertas sunt, et duae bestiae—leo et ursus—introductae sunt cum venatoribus eorum. Leo caudam cito agitabat, ungues in arena imprimens. Ursus autem ponderose ambulavit, sed vultu minaci spectatores intuebatur.

"Ecce, leo tam ferox est!" Tullia clamavit. "Nonne videtis quomodo saevit?"

"Ursus videtur gravior," Aurelia respondit. "Utinam leo vincat. Melior est."

Dum loquebantur, venatores hastas suas levaverunt et circum bestias se moverunt. Leo rugiit et subito in unum venatorem prosiluit. Vir tamen agilis fuit et telo suo animal laesit. Spectatores clamaverunt, manus plaudentes.

"Vide illum ictum!" Aurelia clamavit, oculis fulgentibus. "Quam audax est ille venator!"

"The most handsome?" Marcus responded sarcastically. "Does beauty help them stay alive?"

"Not just beauty," Aurelia added with a smile. "But victory and bravery. Gladiators are strong men."

As they passed through the crowds, the friends saw the massive amphitheatre looming before them. The stone structure was so tall that they had to raise their heads to see the top. Inside, the shouts of the spectators already echoed, as if the battle had already begun.

The friends found seats in the middle section, from where the entire spectacle could be seen clearly. Aurelia and Tullia were burning with anticipation, their eyes fixed on the arena. Rufus and Marcus, however, leaned back, smiling and whispering to each other. Severus sat in silence, his face serious.

Suddenly, a trumpet sounded, and everyone fell silent. A herald entered the arena and shouted in a loud voice: "Citizens of Carthage! The games are now beginning! Gladiators and beasts will fight before you. Watch and enjoy!"

The large gates were opened, and two beasts—a lion and a bear—were led in with their hunters. The lion lashed its tail quickly, digging its claws into the sand of the arena. The bear, on the other hand, walked heavily but stared at the spectators with a menacing gaze.

"Look, the lion is so fierce!" Tullia exclaimed. "Do you see how savage it is?"

"The bear seems more powerful," Aurelia replied. "I hope the lion wins. It's better."

As they spoke, the hunters raised their spears and circled around the beasts. The lion roared and suddenly leapt at one of the hunters. The man, however, was agile and struck the animal with his spear. The spectators shouted, clapping their hands.

"Look at that strike!" Aurelia exclaimed, her eyes shining. "How brave that hunter is!"

Ursus interea in alterum venatorem impetum fecit. Iuvenis territus hastam suam iacere conatus est, sed ursus eum humi proiecit. Clamor spectatorum crevit.

"Quid accidit?" Tullia anxie quaesivit. "Num venator mortuus est?"

"Mortuus?" Rufus risit. "Fortasse. Sed hoc pars spectaculi est, nonne? Hic moriuntur, non in convivio."

Post venationem, gladiatores in arenam descenderunt. Fulgores gladiorum sole micabant dum gladiatores populum salutabant. "Ave, cives Carthaginis!" clamaverunt. "Morituri vos salutamus!"

Certamen coepit, clangore metalli resonante. Gladiatores celeriter movebant, gladios levantes et ictus caventes. Unus gladiator, scuto amplo, alium fortiter pulsavit, eum in humum proiciens. Spectatores clamabant: "Iugula eum! Iugula!"

Aurelia et Tullia simul clamaverunt: "Iugula! Iugula!"

Severus, oculis apertis, sororem spectavit. "Aurelia," inquit, "hoc dicis? Num placet tibi homines interfici?"

"Hoc est spectaculum, Severe!" Aurelia risit. "Nonne pulchrum est? Gladiatores ad hoc parantur. Nonne intellegis?"

Interea gladiator victus in arena iacebat, manum ad praetorem tollens, veniam rogans. Praetor in loco suo sedens signum dedit, et victor gladium suum altum tenuit. Spectatores iterum clamabant.

Dum ludi continuabant, amici magis magisque spectaculo capti sunt. Sole occidente, gladiatores proelium suum finierunt. Turba paulatim discedebat, sed amici lente ambulabant, de pugnis inter se colloquentes.

"Dies hic mirabilis fuit," Tullia dixit, dum Aurelia assensum capite dedit.

"Fortasse," Severus respondit, "sed ego nunc quietem desidero."

"Quam mollis es, Severe!" Aurelia risit. "Nos puellae fortitudinem tibi docere possumus."

Meanwhile, the bear charged at another hunter. The terrified young man tried to throw his spear, but the bear knocked him to the ground. The shouts of the spectators grew louder.

"What happened?" Tullia asked anxiously. "Is the hunter dead?"

"Dead?" Rufus laughed. "Perhaps. But that's part of the spectacle, isn't it? They die here, not at a banquet."

After the hunt, the gladiators descended into the arena. The sunlight gleamed off their swords as the gladiators saluted the crowd. "Hail, citizens of Carthage!" they shouted. "We who are about to die salute you!"

The combat began, with the clash of metal echoing. The gladiators moved quickly, raising their swords and dodging blows. One gladiator, wielding a large shield, struck another forcefully, knocking him to the ground. The spectators shouted: "Kill him! Kill him!"

Aurelia and Tullia shouted together: "Kill him! Kill him!"

Severus, his eyes wide, looked at his sister. "Aurelia," he said, "are you really saying that? Do you enjoy seeing men killed?"

"This is a spectacle, Severus!" Aurelia laughed. "Isn't it magnificent? Gladiators are trained for this. Don't you understand?"

Meanwhile, the defeated gladiator lay in the arena, raising his hand to the praetor, begging for mercy. The praetor, seated in his place, gave the signal, and the victor raised his sword high. The spectators shouted once again.

As the games continued, the friends became more and more engrossed in the spectacle. As the sun set, the gladiators finished their battles. The crowd gradually dispersed, but the friends walked slowly, talking among themselves about the fights.

"This day was marvelous," Tullia said, while Aurelia nodded in agreement.

"Perhaps," Severus replied, "but now I desire some peace."

"How soft you are, Severus!" Aurelia laughed. "We girls can teach you strength!"

"Si exemplum fortitudinis es," Rufus murmurat, "mallem mollis esse."

Omnes riserunt, et post longum diem domum redierunt, sermones de gladiatoribus inter se iterum narrantes.

"If you are an example of strength," Rufus murmured, "I'd rather be soft."

Everyone laughed, and after a long day, they returned home, recounting stories about the gladiators to each other once again.

Amici in Thermis

Die sereno Marcus, Rufus et Severus per vias Carthaginis ambulabant, thermas petentes. Sol leniter viam lapideam calefaciebat, dum Marcus, vultu laeto et gestu amplo, amicis loquebatur: "Nihil melius est quam thermas visitare post longam septimanam," inquit. "Corpus requiescit, mens recreatur. Vera Romae inventio!"

"Et sermones," Rufus subridens respondit. "In thermis semper aliquid novi auditur. Rumores, fabulae, nuntii de civitate—omnia ibi discuntur."

Severus, ut mos erat, gravis manens, respondit: "Non solum sermones, sed et cogitationes. Thermae locus sunt sapientiae. Ibi animus purgatur."

Cum thermas attigissent, portam magnam ingressi sunt, ubi servi eos salutaverunt. "Salvete, domini!" unus ex servis clamavit, manus extendens. "Vestes vestras mihi tradite."

Marcus, tunica iam soluta, risit. "Ecce, viri! Post hanc lavationem me regem sentiam. Haec vita est!"

Rufus, calceos removens, servum intuens subridebat. "Spero meum odorem ferre potes, mi serve. Non semper aqua abundat in insula nostra!"

Servus, vultu imperturbato, tunicas et calceos accipiebat. Severus autem, iam sine verbo vestimenta sua tradens, eos hortatus est: "Properate. Non sumus hic ad iocandum, sed ad corpus animamque recreanda."

In apodyterium ingressi, viderunt multos viros vestes deponentes, risu et clamore resonantes. Atmosphaera illic levior erat. Marcus, circumspiciens, dixit: "Ecce, amici. In thermas ingredimur et omnes curas foris relinquemus. Ubi alibi invenies talem voluptatem?"

Postquam omnia deposuerunt, in frigidarium transierunt. Aqua ibi gelida erat, vapor exhalans super superficiem. Rufus, dum in aquam descendebat, subito exclamavit: "Di immortales! Num haec glaciem tangit? Cur haec poena necessaria est?"

Friends at the Baths

On a clear day, Marcus, Rufus, and Severus walked through the streets of Carthage, heading toward the baths. The sun gently warmed the stone-paved road as Marcus, with a cheerful expression and grand gestures, spoke to his friends: "There's nothing better than visiting the baths after a long week," he said. "The body rests, the mind is refreshed. A true Roman invention!"

"And the conversations," Rufus added with a grin. "You always hear something new at the baths. Rumors, stories, news about the city—everything is learned there."

Severus, as usual, remained serious and replied: "Not just conversations, but also reflections. The baths are a place of wisdom. There, the mind is cleansed."

When they reached the baths, they entered through the grand gate, where slaves greeted them. "Welcome, masters!" one of the slaves called out, extending his hands. "Hand over your clothing to me."

Marcus, already loosening his tunic, laughed. "Look, men! After this bath, I'll feel like a king. This is the life!"

Rufus, removing his sandals, smirked at the slave. "I hope you can handle my scent, my good man. Water isn't always plentiful in our apartment building!"

The slave, his expression unchanging, accepted the tunics and sandals. Severus, already handing over his garments silently, urged them: "Hurry. We're not here to joke, but to refresh body and soul."

As they entered the changing room, they saw many men removing their clothes, the room filled with laughter and chatter. The atmosphere was lighthearted. Marcus, looking around, said: "Look, friends. We're entering the baths, and we're leaving all our worries behind. Where else could you find such pleasure?"

After undressing, they moved to the frigidarium. The water there was icy cold, with steam rising gently from its surface. Rufus, as he descended into the water, suddenly shouted: "Immortal gods! Is this touching ice? Why is this torture necessary?"

Marcus, iam usque ad collum submersus, risit et dixit: "Frigidarium est pro veris viris, non pro mollibus. Num mollis esse vis?"

Severus, in angulo sedens, oculos clausit et leniter respondit: "Aqua frigida corpus vigore implet. Duritia melius nos ad vitam parat."

Cum e frigidario egressi essent, iam rigidi et tremuli, in tepidarium se contulerunt. Atmosphaera ibi lenior erat, calore tepido qui sensus molliebat. Marcus, reclinatus, suspiravit. "Hoc est, amici. Perfectum medium: non nimis calidum, non nimis frigidum."

Rufus assensit, caput reclinans. "Si vinum adesset, hic locus esset caelum."

Severus autem, in locum suum sedens, respondit: "Vinum mentem turbaret. Hic locus est pro tranquillitate, non pro ebrietate."

Cum in calidarium intrassent, vapor calidus eos circumdedit. Marcus in sedem marmoream se collocavit, sudore iam perlatus. "Haec vita est! Cur mundus Romanorum tam fortis est? Quia thermas habent."

Rufus, subridens, respondit: "Fortasse Britannia thermas haberet, etiam illi barbari aliquid discere possent."

Severus, caput movens, respondit: "Britannia non Roma fiet, etiam si thermas accipiat. Natura eorum mutari non potest."

Dum haec loquebantur, Rufus subito aliquem recognovit. "Ecce, Marce!" dixit, digito monstrans. "Nonne ille est Lucius? Amicus noster ex legionibus?"

Marcus, oculos ad eum tollens, subridebat. "Lucius! Vere tu es! Accede, amice!"

Lucius eos agnovit et laeto vultu accessit. "Amici!" exclamavit. "Quam diu est ex quo vos vidi! Quid agitis?"

Marcus, now submerged up to his neck, laughed and said: "The *frigidarium* is for real men, not for the weak. Do you want to be weak?"

Severus, sitting in a corner with his eyes closed, calmly replied: "Cold water fills the body with vigor. Hardship prepares us better for life."

When they emerged from the *frigidarium*, stiff and trembling, they moved into the *tepidarium*. The atmosphere there was gentler, with mild warmth that soothed the senses. Marcus, reclining, sighed. "This is it, friends. The perfect middle ground: not too hot, not too cold."

Rufus agreed, leaning his head back. "If only there were wine, this place would be heaven."

Severus, sitting in his spot, replied: "Wine would cloud the mind. This is a place for tranquility, not drunkenness."

When they entered the *calidarium*, hot steam surrounded them. Marcus settled on a marble seat, already covered in sweat. "This is the life! Why is the Roman world so strong? Because we have the baths."

Rufus, grinning, replied: "Perhaps if Britannia had baths, even those barbarians could learn something."

Severus, shaking his head, responded: "Britannia will never become Rome, even if they acquire baths. Their nature cannot be changed."

As they spoke, Rufus suddenly recognized someone. "Look, Marcus!" he said, pointing with his finger. "Isn't that Lucius? Our friend from the legions?"

Marcus, lifting his eyes to him, smiled. "Lucius! Is it truly you? Come over here, friend!"

Lucius recognized them and approached with a joyful expression. "Friends!" he exclaimed. "How long it has been since I've seen you! How are you doing?"

Marcus eum amplexans respondit: "Nos in Carthagine vivimus, sed tu... cur hic es? Nonne adhuc in exercitu servias?"

Lucius humeros sustulit. "Exercitum tandem reliqui. Multos annos in Britannia militavi, sed nunc domum redii. Tempus erat quiescere."

"Dic nobis de Britannia," Rufus rogavit, curiosus. "Semper audivi illas terras esse barbaras et frigidas."

Lucius risit. "Frigidae, certe. Sed etiam plenae mysteriorum. Silvae sine fine, paludes obscurae, et barbari qui plus sciunt quam credi possit. Sed et violentissimi sunt."

Marcus, oculos micantes, rogavit: "Num eos vicistis?"

"Difficile fuit," Lucius respondit. "Gladii eorum sunt breves, sed pugnandi arte excellunt. Nihil tamen difficilius erat quam hiemem tolerare. Ventus tam fortis erat ut castra nostra saepe eriperet."

Dum Marcus et Rufus avidissime audiunt, Severus, qui diu tacuerat, surrexit. "Vos pergite," dixit. "Historiae bonae sunt, sed tempus me vocat. Aliud agere debeo."

"Severe!" Rufus clamavit, risu suffocatus. "Num Britanniam fugis?"

Severus, subridens, respondit: "Aliquando etiam sapiens scit quando discedendum est." Et, his dictis, per vaporibus plenam thermarum portam egressus est. Marcus et Rufus, tamen, in fabulis Lucii immersi remanserunt, dum Severus per vias Carthaginis solus rediit, cogitationibus suis occupatus.

Marcus, embracing him, replied: "We live in Carthage, but you... why are you here? Aren't you still serving in the army?"

Lucius shrugged his shoulders. "I've finally left the army. I served many years in Britannia, but now I've returned home. It was time to rest."

"Tell us about Britannia," Rufus asked, curious. "I've always heard that land is barbaric and cold."

Lucius laughed. "Cold, certainly. But also full of mysteries. Endless forests, dark swamps, and barbarians who know more than you'd believe. But they are also extremely violent."

Marcus, his eyes gleaming, asked: "Did you conquer them?"

"It was difficult," Lucius replied. "Their swords are short, but they excel in the art of fighting. However, nothing was harder than enduring the winter. The wind was so strong it often destroyed our camps."

While Marcus and Rufus listened eagerly, Severus, who had been silent for a long time, stood up. "You all continue," he said. "The stories are good, but time calls me. I have other things to do."

"Severus!" Rufus shouted, choking with laughter. "Are you fleeing from Britannia?"

Severus, smiling slightly, replied: "Even a wise man knows when it's time to leave." And, with that, he exited through the steamy door of the baths. Marcus and Rufus, however, remained immersed in Lucius's tales, while Severus walked alone through the streets of Carthage, lost in his thoughts.

Dolus Severi

Severus, mente consiliorum plenus et corde celeriter pulsante, per vias Carthaginis festinabat. Calor diei iam recedebat, dum sol paulatim occidens umbras longas super vias proiciebat. "Marcus et Rufus in thermis manent," secum cogitabat, "et ego Aureliam inveniam. Nemo suspicabitur quid inter nos sit."

Vicus ubi amici habitabant iam procul visus erat, et Severus paene cursu appropinquabat. Vultus eius, subridens, laetitiam celabat. "Aurelia me exspectat," sibi dixit. "Hoc momentum nostrum erit."

Cum tandem ad insulam pervenisset, ianuam apertam invenit et tacite ingressus est. Cubiculum Aureliae prope erat. Severus alte respiravit, se componens. Ianua paulum aperta erat; Aureliam vocare voluit, sed primo auscultavit. Silentium.

"Aurelia," susurravit, dum cubiculum lente intrabat. Sed prope lectum non Aureliam invenit, sed Tulliam, quae solitaria sedebat, mentum manu sustinens. Vultus eius paene somnolentus erat, sed oculi statim in Severum fixi sunt, cum eum vidit.

"Severe," inquit, subridens. "Cur ita festinas? Nonne Marcus et Rufus tecum sunt?"

Severus, vultu leviter confuso, respondit: "Aliquid urgente abii. Sed... cur tu sola es? Ubi est Aurelia?"

Tullia humeros levavit, dissimulans. "Aurelia foris abiit. Ego sola hic remansi. Hic locus mihi videbatur... taediosus." Paulum inclinata, lentum risum addidit: "Nunc autem tu advenisti. Fortasse taedium meum finias."

"Ego," Severus coepit, sed verba eius quasi haeserunt. Non placuit ei manere, sed Tullia eum oculis quasi captavit. "Ego paulisper manebo," tandem dixit, lente sedens prope eam. "Sed tempus breve est."

Tullia, vultu leniter provocante, propius accessit. "Cur tam rigidus es? Me timesne, Severe?"

Severus's Scheme

Severus, his mind full of plans and his heart racing, hurried through the streets of Carthage. The heat of the day was fading as the slowly setting sun cast long shadows over the streets. "Marcus and Rufus are staying in the baths," he thought to himself, "and I will find Aurelia. No one will suspect what might happen between us."

The neighborhood where his friends lived was already in sight, and Severus was approaching at almost a run. His face, smiling, concealed his excitement. "Aurelia awaits me," he said to himself. "This will be our moment."

When he finally reached the apartment building, he found the door ajar and quietly stepped inside. Aurelia's room was nearby. Severus took a deep breath, steadying himself. The door was slightly open; he wanted to call out to Aurelia but first decided to listen. Silence.

"Aurelia," he whispered as he slowly entered the room. But near the bed, he didn't find Aurelia—instead, he found Tullia sitting alone, her chin resting on her hand. Her expression was almost drowsy, but her eyes immediately fixed on Severus as soon as she saw him.

"Severus," she said, smiling. "Why are you in such a hurry? Aren't Marcus and Rufus with you?"

Severus, his expression slightly confused, replied: "Something urgent came up, so I left. But... why are you alone? Where is Aurelia?"

Tullia shrugged, feigning indifference. "Aurelia went out. I stayed here alone. This place seemed... boring to me." Leaning forward slightly, she added with a slow smile: "But now you've arrived. Perhaps you'll end my boredom."

"I..." Severus began, but his words seemed to stick. He didn't want to stay, but Tullia's gaze seemed to hold him captive. "I'll stay for a little while," he finally said, sitting down slowly near her. "But only for a short time."

Tullia, her expression gently teasing, moved closer. "Why are you so stiff? Are you afraid of me, Severus?"

"Non timeo," Severus graviter respondit. "Sed ego... aliud cogitabam."

"Aliud?" Tullia subridens respondit, manum suam lente super eius brachium ponens. "Num ego tam parvi momenti sum, ut tu alibi sis mente tua?"

Severus respicere conatus est, sed oculi eius ad Tulliam traxerunt. "Tullia," dixit, paulum tremens, "ego... hoc non decet."

"Non decet?" Tullia susurravit, paulo propius inclinans. "Quid est, Severe, quod vere vis?"

Severus, quem semper ratio moderabatur, hoc tempore ardebat. "Tullia, ego—" Verba eius interclusa sunt, cum labia sua labia eius tetigerunt. Brevi momento nihil aliud exsistebat nisi calor passionis.

Tullia, risu molli, eum ad lectum traxit. "Videsne?" inquit. "Nonne hoc melius est quam sermones graves?"

Severus nihil respondit, sed manum suam sub vestimento eius posuit, dum cor eius celerius quam umquam ante pulsabat. "Tullia..." coepit, sed subito strepitus auditus est. Ianua cubiculi violenter aperta est.

"Aurelia!" clamavit Severus, subito exsurgens, vultu pallente. Ante eos Aurelia stabat, vultu irae plenissimo. Manus eius ad latera tensae erant, et oculi quasi fulmina emiserunt.

"Severe!" Aurelia exclamavit. "Quid hic agis? Et tu, Tullia? Quid vultis? Hoc—hoc incredibile est!"

Tullia, composita sed provocans, lente surrexit. "Cur tam irata es, Aurelia?" inquit, subridens. "Severus non tuus est. Num quid promisit?"

"Promisit?" Aurelia voce tremens respondit. "Tullia, tu es perfida! Et tu, Severe, quam facile oblivisceris quid inter nos fuerit!"

Severus verba quaerens caput movit. "Aurelia, ego... hoc non ita fuit. Nihil significavit."

"I am not afraid," Severus replied gravely. "But I... I was thinking of something else."

"Something else?" Tullia responded with a sly smile, slowly placing her hand on his arm. "Am I so insignificant that your mind is elsewhere?"

Severus tried to look away, but his eyes were drawn to Tullia. "Tullia," he said, trembling slightly, "this isn't right."

"Not right?" Tullia whispered, leaning closer. "What is it, Severus, that you truly want?"

Severus, usually ruled by reason, was now consumed by emotion. "Tullia, I—" His words were cut off as her lips touched his. For a brief moment, nothing existed but the heat of passion.

Tullia, with a soft laugh, pulled him toward the bed. "See?" she said. "Isn't this better than serious conversations?"

Severus said nothing, but his hand moved under her garment as his heart raced faster than ever before. "Tullia..." he began, but suddenly a noise interrupted them. The door to the room burst open violently.

"Aurelia!" Severus exclaimed, springing to his feet, his face pale. In the doorway stood Aurelia, her face full of fury. Her hands were clenched at her sides, and her eyes seemed to shoot lightning.

"Severus!" Aurelia shouted. "What are you doing here? And you, Tullia? What do you both want? This—this is unbelievable!"

Tullia, composed but defiant, rose slowly. "Why are you so angry, Aurelia?" she said with a smile. "Severus is not yours. Did he make you any promises?"

"Promises?" Aurelia replied, her voice trembling. "Tullia, you are a traitor! And you, Severus, how easily you forget what we had between us!"

Severus, searching for words, shook his head. "Aurelia, I... it wasn't like that. It meant nothing."

"Nihil significavit?" Aurelia clamavit, manu ad Tulliam extendens quasi eam pulsare vellet. "Tu me tam stultam putas? Ego omnia vidi!"

Tullia, manibus in latera posita, subridens dixit: "Cur non tranquillam te praebes, Aurelia? Nonne hoc iam evenire sciebas? Severus non est vir fidelis."

"Aperi os tuum iterum," Aurelia irata dixit, "et ego te verberabo!"

"Proba, si audes," Tullia respondit, vultu provocante.

Clamor earum totum conclave implebat. Severus, inter duas furias inclusus, paulatim retrocessit, manus in caput ponens. "Placate vos!" clamavit. "Haec nihil boni affert!"

"Tacere debes, Severe!" Aurelia respondit, oculos igneos in eum figens. "Tu es qui nos in hoc deduxisti!"

"Tu ipse voluisti," Tullia addidit, oculis sardonicis. "Nemo te coegit."

Cum clamores crescere videret et pax impossibilis appareret, Severus tandem ad ianuam cubiculi se retraxit. "Ambae insanitis," murmuravit. "Nihil hic maneo." Subito per ianuam discessit, dum voces eorum post eum resonabant.

In vias Carthaginis se iactavit, vultu confuso et corde gravato. "Hoc non debuit fieri," sibi dixit. "Quid nunc agam?" Et, caput inclinans, lente ambulavit in noctem silentem.

"Meant nothing?" Aurelia shouted, extending her hand toward Tullia as if she were about to strike her. "Do you think I'm that stupid? I saw everything!"

Tullia, placing her hands on her hips and smiling, said: "Why don't you calm yourself, Aurelia? Didn't you already know this would happen? Severus isn't a faithful man."

"Open your mouth again," Aurelia said angrily, "and I'll hit you!"

"Try, if you dare," Tullia replied, her expression defiant.

Their shouting filled the entire room. Severus, caught between the two furies, slowly backed away, putting his hands on his head. "Calm yourselves!" he shouted. "This is helping no one!"

"You should be silent, Severus!" Aurelia responded, fixing her fiery gaze on him. "You're the one who dragged us into this!"

"You wanted this yourself," Tullia added with a sardonic look. "No one forced you."

As the shouting grew louder and peace seemed impossible, Severus finally retreated toward the door of the room. "You're both insane," he muttered. "I'm not staying here." Suddenly, he slipped out through the door, their voices echoing behind him.

He threw himself onto the streets of Carthage, his face confused and his heart heavy. "This shouldn't have happened," he said to himself. "What do I do now?" And, lowering his head, he walked slowly into the silent night.

Severus et Latrones

Severus, post tumultum in insula, per vias Carthaginis vagabatur, mente turbata et corde gravi. Nox iam ceciderat, et luna inter nubes rara lucebat. Umbrae longae per vias desertas serpentes Severum sequebantur, dum tardis passibus in silentio ambulabat.

"Quid nunc faciam?" secum murmuravit, vultu graviter inclinato. "Aurelia et Tullia ambae me oderunt. Quomodo hanc stultitiam corrigam?"

Dum cogitabat, ex proximo vico subito clamores auditi sunt. Vox plena terroris resonabat, et Severus statim substitit, auribus intentis. "Adiuvate!" aliquis clamavit. "Latrones!"

Severus oculos ad tenebras vertit et sine mora currere coepit versus clamores. Cum ad locum pervenisset, vidit Rufum et Marcum cum tribus viris pugnantibus. Duo latrones gladios vibrabant, dum tertius, vir robustus et immanis, Rufum ad terram prostraverat et cultrum super pectus eius levaverat.

"Di immortales!" Severus exclamavit. Sine dubitatione in proelium irruit. Lapidem de via celeriter arripiens, illum in latronem fortem iecit. Latro, ictu attonitus, cultrum suum subito demisit et retrocedere coactus est.

Rufus, adhuc humi iacens, exclamavit: "Severe! Per deos, adiuvato nos!"

Severus gladium quem latro amiserat arripuit et contra alium latronem se vertit. "Abite!" clamavit, gladium vibrans. "Nisi fugitis, vos interficiam!"

Latrones, nunc animo trepidantes, per momenta pugnam continuaverunt, sed Severus cum Marco et Rufo fortiter se defendebant. Postquam unus latro vulneratus est, reliqui duo, pavidi, clamores emiserunt et per vias obscuras fugerunt.

Marcus, anhelans et sudore perlatus, gladium in terram demisit. "Severe," ait, "tu nos servavisti. Si non venisses, Rufus certe mortuus esset."

Severus and the Bandits

Severus, after the commotion in the apartment building, wandered through the streets of Carthage, his mind troubled and his heart heavy. Night had fallen, and the moon shone faintly between the clouds. Long shadows snaked along the deserted streets, following Severus as he walked slowly in silence.

"What do I do now?" he murmured to himself, his face deeply bowed. "Both Aurelia and Tullia hate me. How can I fix this foolishness?"

While he was deep in thought, sudden shouts rang out from a nearby alley. A voice full of terror echoed, and Severus immediately stopped, straining his ears. "Help!" someone cried. "Bandits!"

Severus turned his eyes toward the darkness and, without hesitation, began running toward the shouts. When he arrived at the scene, he saw Rufus and Marcus fighting with three men. Two of the bandits were wielding swords, while the third, a large and imposing man, had knocked Rufus to the ground and was raising a dagger over his chest.

"Immortal gods!" Severus exclaimed. Without hesitation, he rushed into the fray. Grabbing a stone from the street, he hurled it at the burly bandit. The bandit, stunned by the blow, dropped his dagger and staggered backward.

Rufus, still lying on the ground, shouted: "Severus! By the gods, help us!"

Severus picked up the sword the bandit had dropped and turned toward another attacker. "Get away!" he shouted, brandishing the sword. "If you don't flee, I'll kill you!"

The bandits, now filled with hesitation, continued the fight for a few moments, but Severus, alongside Marcus and Rufus, fought back fiercely. After one bandit was wounded, the remaining two, frightened, cried out and fled into the dark streets.

Marcus, panting and drenched in sweat, dropped his sword to the ground. "Severus," he said, "you saved us. If you hadn't come, Rufus would surely be dead."

Rufus, adhuc humi sedens, vultu pallido et sanguinem e naribus tergens, aspiciens Severum, susurravit: "Gratias tibi ago, Severe. Tu es... verus amicus."

Severus, gladium procul iacens, ad Rufum accessit et eum sublevavit. "Non potui vos relinquere," dixit. "Sed quid hic agebatis, soli in tenebris?"

"Lucium comitabamur," Marcus respondit, "sed, cum illum dimisissent, viam breviorem domum eligimus. Tum latrones nos aggressi sunt."

Post breve silentium Marcus Severum aspexit, vultu subridens. "At tu, Severe, quid hic agebas? Nonne in insula eras?"

Severus vultum avertit, paulum rubescens. "Ego..." coepit, sed Rufus, iam paulo melior, eum impulit: "Dic nobis! Num aliquid accidit?"

Severus, suspirans et caput inclinans, respondit: "Confiteor. Dum vos in thermis eratis, domum redii... et Tulliam inveni. Primo nolui manere, sed illa me provocavit. Nos... nos osculati sumus."

Marcus, iratus, subito clamavit: "Tullia? Tullia? Et quid de Aurelia? Num omnino stultus es?"

Rufus autem, vultu leniore, manum in brachium Severi posuit. "Satis," ait. "Severus, stulte egisti, sed omnes erramus. Ego tibi ignosco."

Marcus, adhuc fremens, caput movit et in viam despexit. "Bene, Rufus. Si tu potes ignoscere, et ego possum. Sed Severus, promitte te melius cogitaturum in posterum."

"Promitto," Severus graviter respondit. "Hoc numquam iterum fiet."

Rufus subridebat et in pectus Severi manum leviter percussit. "Nunc autem, amici, tempus est vinum bibere. Meremur."

Marcus risit, paulum mollitus. "Bene dixisti, Rufe. In tabernam eamus. Hodie vivimus!"

Rufus, still sitting on the ground, pale and wiping blood from his nose, looked up at Severus and whispered: "Thank you, Severus. You are... a true friend."

Severus, tossing the sword aside, approached Rufus and helped him up. "I couldn't leave you," he said. "But what were you doing here, alone in the dark?"

"We were escorting Lucius," Marcus replied, "but after he was released, we chose a shorter way home. Then the bandits attacked us."

After a brief silence, Marcus looked at Severus, smiling slightly. "But you, Severus, what were you doing here? Weren't you at the apartment?"

Severus turned his face away, blushing slightly. "I..." he began, but Rufus, feeling a little better, nudged him: "Tell us! Did something happen?"

Severus sighed and lowered his head. "I confess. While you were at the baths, I went back home... and found Tullia. At first, I didn't want to stay, but she provoked me. We... we kissed."

Marcus, furious, suddenly shouted: "Tullia? Tullia? And what about Aurelia? Are you completely stupid?"

Rufus, however, with a calmer expression, placed a hand on Severus's arm. "Enough," he said. "Severus, you acted foolishly, but we all make mistakes. I forgive you."

Marcus, still fuming, shook his head and looked down at the road. "Fine, Rufus. If you can forgive him, so can I. But Severus, promise you'll think more clearly in the future."

"I promise," Severus replied solemnly. "This will never happen again."

Rufus smiled and lightly patted Severus on the chest. "Now then, friends, it's time to drink some wine. We've earned it."

Marcus laughed, his anger softening. "Well said, Rufus. Let's go to the tavern. Today, we live!"

Tabernam invenerunt prope forum, ubi adhuc pauci homines sedebant, vino fruentes. Severus, Marcus, et Rufus mensam in angulo elegerunt et amphoram vini iusserunt. Post primum poculum, sermo levior factus est.

"Num recordamini," Marcus, iam paululum ebrius, dixit, "quando Severus philosophus esse volebat? Et nunc latrones fugat et puellas osculatur!"

Rufus risit, poculum suum attollens. "Euge, Severe! Vere vir varius es."

"Tacete, ambo," Severus respondit, sed subridebat. "Vos vinum nimis bibitis."

Post plura pocula, omnes ridebant, cantabant, et curas noctis obliviscebantur. Cum tandem tabernam reliquissent, per vias titubantes ambulaverunt. Marcus, iterum risu interruptus, dixit: "Haec nox certe memorabilis est. Sed cras... caput dolebis, Severe."

"Cras de dolore cogitabo," Severus murmurat, iam paene dormiens.

Cum domum pervenissent, unus post alterum in lectos suos collapsi sunt. Noctis silentium eos circumdedit, et omnes in somno profundo quieverunt.

They found a tavern near the forum, where a few people were still sitting, enjoying their wine. Severus, Marcus, and Rufus chose a table in the corner and ordered a pitcher of wine. After the first cup, the mood lightened.

"Do you remember," Marcus, already a little drunk, said, "when Severus wanted to be a philosopher? And now he's chasing off bandits and kissing girls!"

Rufus laughed, raising his cup. "Bravo, Severus! Truly, you're a man of many talents."

"Be quiet, both of you," Severus replied, though he smiled. "You've had too much wine."

After several more cups, they were all laughing, singing, and forgetting the troubles of the night. When they finally left the tavern, they staggered through the streets. Marcus, laughing again, said: "This night is certainly unforgettable. But tomorrow... you'll have a headache, Severus."

"I'll think about the pain tomorrow," Severus murmured, already half-asleep.

When they reached home, they collapsed one after the other into their beds. The silence of the night surrounded them, and they all rested in deep sleep.

Aurelia et Tullia in Foro Carthaginis

Aurora prima luce Carthaginem perstrinxerat, dum Aurelia et Tullia, vestibus simplicibus indutae, per vias fori ambulabant. Sol in summo caelo lente oriebatur, et clamor venditorum iam aerem implebat: "Poma recentia! Olea optima! Vinum dulce!"

"Nonne mirabile est, Tullia?" Aurelia dixit, oculos circa se movens. "Tot res hic sunt. Vellem nos plures nummos haberemus."

Tullia risit, humeros tollens. "Fortasse divitias non habemus, sed spectare certe nihil constat."

Per fori spatium ambulabant, ubi tabernae omnia genera mercium offerebant. In una taberna vir robustus, toga sordida, amphoras vini ostendebat. "Hoc vinum de Sicilia venit!" clamavit. "Dulcius est quam nectar deorum!"

Aurelia, oculis micantibus, ad tabernam accessit. "Vinum pulchre olere videtur," inquit, manus extendens quasi amphoram tangere vellet.

"Pulchre quidem olet," Tullia respondit, manum Aureliae trahens. "Sed pretium certe nimis altum est pro nobis. Procedamus."

Paulo post ad aliam tabernam pervenerunt, ubi mulier cana, vultu amabili, corbes plenos pomorum et nucum vendebat. "Poma recentia!" clamavit. "Nucae dulcissimae! Hodie omnes pretio bono accipiunt!"

Aurelia poma rubra conspexit et susurravit: "Vellem unam emere. Vide quam pulchra sint!"

"Nummos tuos numera, Aurelia," Tullia subridens respondit. "Si unum pomum emeris, num aliquid reliquum erit pro cena?"

Aurelia suspiravit, sed manus a pomis retraxit. "Recte dicis. Sed olim dives ero, et haec omnia emam!" Subito ridens adiecit: "Et tibi nihil dabo."

"Gratias, mea cara," Tullia respondit, risu molli. "Tunc ego aliam amicam divitem quaeram."

Aurelia and Tullia in the Forum of Carthage

The first light of dawn brushed over Carthage as Aurelia and Tullia, dressed in simple clothes, walked through the bustling streets of the forum. The sun was slowly rising in the sky, and the cries of vendors were already filling the air: "Fresh fruit! The finest olives! Sweet wine!"

"Isn't it wonderful, Tullia?" Aurelia said, looking around. "There are so many things here. I wish we had more coins."

Tullia laughed, shrugging her shoulders. "Perhaps we don't have riches, but looking certainly costs nothing."

They walked across the forum, where the stalls offered all kinds of goods. At one stall, a burly man in a dirty toga was displaying amphoras of wine. "This wine comes from Sicily!" he shouted. "It's sweeter than the nectar of the gods!"

Aurelia, her eyes gleaming, approached the stall. "The wine seems to smell wonderful," she said, reaching out as if to touch an amphora.

"It does smell wonderful," Tullia replied, pulling Aurelia's hand back. "But I'm sure the price is far too high for us. Let's move on."

A little later, they arrived at another stall, where an elderly woman with a kind face was selling baskets full of fruit and nuts. "Fresh fruit!" she called out. "The sweetest nuts! Everything is available at a good price today!"

Aurelia noticed the bright red apples and whispered: "I wish I could buy one. Look how beautiful they are!"

"Count your coins, Aurelia," Tullia replied with a smile. "If you buy one apple, will there be anything left for dinner?"

Aurelia sighed but pulled her hand back from the apples. "You're right. But one day I'll be rich, and I'll buy all of this!" Then, laughing, she added: "And I won't give you anything."

"Thank you, my dear," Tullia replied with a soft laugh. "Then I'll find myself another rich friend."

Dum per forum ambulabant, ad tabernam ornamentorum pervenerunt, ubi venditor iuvenis anulos et armillas argenteas ostentabat. "Veni, specta!" clamavit. "Haec armilla te pulchriorem faciet quam Venus ipsa!"

Aurelia, oculis micantibus, ad tabernam properavit. "Tullia, vide! Quam mirabilis est iste anulus cum gemma caerulea!"

Venditor, vultu callido, anulum sustulit. "Haec gemma de Nilo venit," dixit. "Nulla mulier tam splendida erit nisi hunc anulum gerat."

"Quantus est?" Aurelia rogavit, sperans pretium fortasse non esse nimium.

"Octo denarii," venditor respondit, subridens.

Tullia risit et Aureliam a taberna retraxit. "Octo denarii? Fortasse si latronem divitem invenias! Procedamus, Aurelia. Nos vinum nec gemmas comparare possumus."

"Sed pulcherrimus erat," Aurelia murmurat, paulum trahens.

Ad tabernam panis pervenerunt, ubi panis calidus ex fornace recentissime eductus erat. Odores delectabiles aerem implebant, et venditor clamitabat: "Panis mollis! Panis calidus! Perfectus pro cena vestra!"

"Saltem panem emere possumus," Tullia dixit, nummos ex sacculo suo numerans. "Quanti sunt duo panes?"

"Duo asses," venditor respondit, eos panem fragranti odore tentans.

"Euge," Tullia respondit, nummos porrigens. "Hoc certe valde melius est quam gemmae quae nec famem tollunt nec ventrem replent."

"Panem habemus," Aurelia subridens dixit, panem calidum manibus stringens. "Sed quid de caseo vel ficis?"

As they walked through the forum, they came upon a jewelry stall where a young vendor was displaying silver rings and bracelets. "Come, take a look!" he called out. "This bracelet will make you more beautiful than Venus herself!"

Aurelia, her eyes gleaming, hurried to the stall. "Tullia, look! How marvelous is that ring with the blue gem!"

The vendor, with a cunning expression, lifted the ring. "This gem comes from the Nile," he said. "No woman will be as magnificent unless she wears this ring."

"How much is it?" Aurelia asked, hoping the price might not be too high.

"Eight denarii," the vendor replied with a smile.

Tullia laughed and pulled Aurelia away from the stall. "Eight denarii? Perhaps if you find a rich bandit! Let's move on, Aurelia. We can't afford wine, let alone gems."

"But it was so beautiful," Aurelia murmured, dragging her feet slightly.

They arrived at a bread stall, where warm loaves had just been taken from the oven. Delicious smells filled the air, and the vendor was shouting: "Soft bread! Warm bread! Perfect for your dinner!"

"At least we can afford bread," Tullia said, counting coins from her pouch. "How much for two loaves?"

"Two asses," the vendor replied, tempting them with the fragrant aroma of the bread.

"Excellent," Tullia said, handing over the coins. "This is certainly much better than gems that neither ease hunger nor fill the stomach."

"We have bread," Aurelia said with a smile, squeezing the warm loaf in her hands. "But what about cheese or figs?"

Tullia humeros levavit. "Si magis emere velis, nummos tuos adde. Meae divitiae iam exhaustae sunt."

Perrexerunt ad tabernam ubi ficus et olivas vendebant. Aurelia, paulum dubitans, unum assium porrexit et corbem parvam ficuum accepit. "Saltem hoc," inquit, ficum unam gustans. "Dulcissima est."

Forum paulatim replebatur, et clamor venditorum crescebat. Vir quidam iuvenis, cum herbis aromaticis, accessit et Tulliam allocutus est: "Pulchra domina, num odores hos tibi placent?"

Tullia, oculos volvens, respondit: "Odor placet, sed nummi non sufficiunt. Gratias tibi ago, bone vir."

Cum multa spectata essent sed parum emptum, Aurelia et Tullia tandem domum redierunt, panem et ficus manibus portantes. Aurelia, paulum anhelans, dixit: "Quam mirabile est forum, sed dives esse necesse est ut omnia vera frui possis."

"Vere dixisti," Tullia respondit, subridens. "Sed saltem cena nostra erit bona. Et gemmae nobis non necessariae sunt, nonne?"

"Forsitan," Aurelia respondit, sed oculis micantibus adiecit: "Tamen, aliquando gemmam illam habebo."

Ridentes domum pervenerunt, contentae, sed secreta spe divitias futuras optantes.

Tullia shrugged her shoulders. "If you want to buy more, add your own coins. My wealth is already exhausted."

They continued to a stall where figs and olives were sold. Aurelia, hesitating slightly, handed over one *as* and received a small basket of figs. "At least this," she said, tasting one. "It's so sweet."

The forum gradually grew busier, and the shouts of vendors became louder. A young man selling aromatic herbs approached and addressed Tullia: "Beautiful lady, do these scents please you?"

Tullia, rolling her eyes, replied: "The scent is pleasant, but my coins are insufficient. Thank you, kind sir."

After seeing much but buying little, Aurelia and Tullia finally returned home, carrying bread and figs in their hands. Aurelia, slightly out of breath, said: "The forum is so wonderful, but you must be rich to truly enjoy everything it offers."

"You speak the truth," Tullia replied, smiling. "But at least our dinner will be good. And we don't really need gems, do we?"

"Perhaps," Aurelia replied, but with her eyes gleaming, she added: "Still, one day I'll have that gem."

Laughing, they returned home, content but secretly hoping for future riches.

Marcus in Fullonica Carthaginis

Solis radii crudeliter ardebant, dum Marcus in angusto vico Carthaginis, sudore perlatus, laborabat. Aer erat calidus et gravis, plenus odore acri, qui a fullonica proxima emanabat. Fullonica erat locus ubi panni purgabantur et tingebantur; opus grave, sordidum, et ingrato odore plenum.

Marcus amphoram plenam lotii portabat, quod a viatoribus in amphoras publicas collectum erat. Urina in fullonica ad pelles tingendas et pannos purgandos utebatur. Marcus, vultu maesto sed cogitationibus alio loco vagantibus, per viam titubabat.

"Quam dura est vita mea," murmurat sibi. "Cur ego semper miseros labores facio? Quid si dives mercator essem, togam candidam gerens et aurum possidens? Forsitan…"

Subito Marcus in imaginationibus suis tam alte immersus fuit ut lapidem in via non videret. Cum pede eum offenderet, amphoram quam manibus tenebat non tenuit. Amphora fragore terribili in pavimentum fracta est, et lotium, quod intus erat, ubique effusum est.

Marcus statim palluit. "O di immortales," sibilavit. "Quid feci?"

Antequam se colligere poterat, clamor ex latere auditus est. "Esne demens?!" magna voce clamavit mercator dives, toga splendida et ornamento aureo insignis. Lotium, quod effusum erat, iam in togam suam infundebatur. Vultus eius, qui primo fastidiosus erat, nunc ira plenus factus est.

"Tu, stulte!" clamavit mercator, digito Marcum monstrans. "Nonne oculos habes? Quomodo audes me inquinare?"

Marcus, qui iam tremebat, conatus est loqui. "Domine… ignosce… casu accidit. Non volui…"

"Non voluisti?" mercator interrupit, voce plena irae. "Nonne scis quid mea toga valeat? Haec est lana purpurea, de Tyro importata! Tu meum honorem et togam meam violavisti!"

Marcus in the Fuller's Workshop of Carthage

The cruel rays of the sun burned down as Marcus labored through a narrow street in Carthage, drenched in sweat. The air was hot and heavy, filled with a sharp odor emanating from a nearby fullonica. The fullonica was a place where cloth was cleaned and dyed—a harsh, dirty, and foul-smelling job.

Marcus was carrying a full amphora of urine, collected from public jars by passersby. Urine was used in the fullonica for tanning hides and cleaning cloth. With a gloomy expression, but his thoughts wandering elsewhere, Marcus stumbled along the road.

"How hard my life is," he murmured to himself. "Why must I always do such miserable work? What if I were a rich merchant, wearing a white toga and owning gold? Perhaps…"

Suddenly, Marcus, so deeply immersed in his daydreams, didn't notice a stone in the road. When his foot struck it, he lost his grip on the amphora he was holding. With a terrible crash, the amphora shattered on the pavement, and the urine inside spilled everywhere.

Marcus immediately turned pale. "Immortal gods," he hissed. "What have I done?"

Before he could collect himself, a shout came from the side. "Are you insane?!" cried a loud voice. A wealthy merchant, dressed in a splendid toga adorned with gold ornaments, stood there. The spilled urine had already soaked into his toga. His face, initially showing disdain, now burned with anger.

"You fool!" the merchant shouted, pointing at Marcus. "Don't you have eyes? How dare you soil me?"

Marcus, now trembling, tried to speak. "Sir… forgive me… it was an accident. I didn't mean to—"

"Didn't mean to?" the merchant interrupted, his voice filled with rage. "Don't you know what my toga is worth? This is purple wool, imported from Tyre! You've insulted my honor and ruined my toga!"

Alia vox e fullonica audita est. Dominus officinae, vir pinguis et vultu gravi, processit. "Quid hic fit?" rogavit, vultu confuso. Cum amphoram fractam et lotium dispersum vidit, vultus eius nigrior factus est.

"Dominus tuus?" mercator quaesivit, ad pinguis virum versus. "Si hic puer tuus est, tibi illum statim dimittere suadeo! Turpem ac negligentem habes operarium!"

Dominus officinae, vultu iam irato, Marcum aspexit. "Marce!" clamavit. "Quid fecisti? Nonne dixi tibi ut curares? Tu non solum lotium perdidisti, sed etiam honorem meum coram hoc domino divite!"

Marcus, iam confusus et humilitatus, manibus apertis conatus est explicare. "Non volui, domine. Lapidem offenderam. Amphora ex manibus meis lapsa est…"

"Lapsa est?" dominus fremuit. "Tu semper excusas invenis, Marcus. Hoc non est primum, nec ultimum. Ego te dimitto!"

"Dimittis?" Marcus, oculis plenis desperationis, exclamavit. "Domine, quaeso… mihi opus est hoc labore. Non habeo aliam pecuniam. Familia mea esurit!"

Dominus tamen caput movit, vultu duro. "Mea patientia finita est, Marcus. Hoc non est negotium misericordiae. Egredere statim!"

Marcus, vultu confuso et oculis demissis, paulum titubavit. Tandem, verba amplius invenire non potuit. Domini iussu, ex fullonica discessit, dum mercator et dominus clamoribus suis eum prosequebantur.

Cum per vias Carthaginis errabat, vultu moesto, sudore et odore lotii plenus, secum murmuravit: "Cur fortuna semper adversa mihi est? Cur dives non sum, sed pauper, semper humi iacens?"

Marcus tandem sub arbore parva prope forum consedit, lacrimas continere conatus. Calor diei nondum defecerat, sed spes eius, quae numquam magna fuerat, nunc penitus fracta erat.

Another voice was heard from the *fuller's workshop*. The master of the workshop, a fat man with a stern expression, stepped forward. "What is happening here?" he asked, looking puzzled. When he saw the shattered amphora and the urine spilled everywhere, his face darkened further.

"Is this your servant?" the merchant demanded, turning toward the fat man. "If he is your worker, I strongly advise you to dismiss him immediately! You employ someone careless and disgraceful!"

The workshop master, now visibly angry, glared at Marcus. "Marcus!" he shouted. "What have you done? Didn't I tell you to be careful? You've not only wasted the urine but also disgraced me in front of this wealthy merchant!"

Marcus, already embarrassed and humiliated, raised his hands, trying to explain. "I didn't mean to, master. I tripped over a stone. The amphora slipped from my hands…"

"Slipped?" the master growled. "You always have excuses, Marcus. This isn't the first time, and it won't be the last. You're dismissed!"

"Dismissed?" Marcus exclaimed, his eyes filled with desperation. "Master, please… I need this job. I have no other money. My family is starving!"

The master, however, shook his head with a stern expression. "My patience is at its end, Marcus. This isn't a charity. Leave immediately!"

Marcus, his face crestfallen and his eyes downcast, hesitated for a moment. In the end, he could find no more words. At the master's command, he left the *fuller's workshop*, as the merchant and the master continued to shout after him.

As he wandered through the streets of Carthage, his face sad, his clothes soaked in sweat and reeking of urine, he murmured to himself: "Why is fortune always against me? Why am I not rich, but instead poor, always brought to the ground?"

Finally, Marcus sat beneath a small tree near the forum, trying to hold back tears. The heat of the day had not yet faded, but his hope, which had never been great, was now completely shattered.

Marcus et Amici: Fabula de Lotio

In angusto conclavi insulae Carthaginis amici congregati erant: Severus, Rufus, Aurelia, Tullia, et Marcus, qui nuper domum redierat vultu tristi sed oculis quibusdam furtive micantibus. Sol iam occiderat, et lumen parvae lucernae umbras in parietes proiectabat.

"Marcus," Rufus clamavit, dum in scamno inclinatus panem frangit, "quid accidit? Cur ita moerens videris? Nonne in fullonica bene tibi erat?"

Marcus suspiravit et sedit, manibus caput tenens. "O amici," inquit, "hodie mala fortuna me persequebatur. Opus meum perdidi!"

"Opus perdidisti?" Tullia exclamavit, oculis sublatis. "Quid fecisti?"

"Dic nobis!" Severus graviter interposuit, ut mos ei erat. "Nonne tibi mandatum erat amphoras curare et diligentiam servare?"

Marcus humeros levavit, quasi causam explicare vix posset. "Amphoram portabam, ut mos est in fullonica, plenam lotii—"

"Lotii?" Aurelia ridens interrupit. "Pro di immortales, Marcus! Quomodo possis cum tali odore vivere?"

"Odore vivere?" Marcus respondit, vultu paulum indignato. "Tu non scis quantum grave sit opus meum! Quid autem feci? Cogitabam de vita, de fortuna, de—fortasse de divitiis—"

"Ah," Rufus risit, poculum suum levans. "Marcus philosophus! Certe, dum cogitabas de fortuna, lotium effundisti, nonne?"

"Quasi ita!" Marcus clamavit, manus in aerem tollens. "Subito lapidem offenderam, et amphora ex manibus meis elapsa est. Fragor terribilis factus est!"

"Et quid tum accidit?" Severus quaesivit, vultu immoto. "Nonne tantum lotium humum infudit?"

"Utinam ita fuisset," Marcus murmurat. "Sed, o amici, mercator dives ibi stabat—"

Marcus and Friends: The Tale of the Urine

In the cramped apartment of the Carthaginian insula, the friends had gathered: Severus, Rufus, Aurelia, Tullia, and Marcus, who had just returned home with a sorrowful expression but a certain furtive glint in his eyes. The sun had already set, and the dim light of a small oil lamp cast shadows on the walls.

"Marcus," Rufus called out, leaning on a bench as he broke some bread, "what happened? Why do you look so gloomy? Wasn't everything going well at the fullonica?"

Marcus sighed and sat down, holding his head in his hands. "Oh, my friends," he said, "today misfortune pursued me. I lost my job!"

"You lost your job?" Tullia exclaimed, her eyes widening. "What did you do?"

"Tell us!" Severus interjected seriously, as was his habit. "Weren't you tasked with taking care of the amphoras and being careful?"

Marcus shrugged, as if he could barely explain himself. "I was carrying an amphora, as usual in the fullonica, full of urine—"

"Urine?" Aurelia interrupted, laughing. "By the immortal gods, Marcus! How can you live with such a smell?"

"Live with the smell?" Marcus replied, his expression slightly offended. "You have no idea how hard my work is! But what did I do? I was thinking about life, about fortune, about—perhaps about wealth—"

"Ah," Rufus laughed, raising his cup. "Marcus the philosopher! Of course, while you were thinking about fortune, you spilled the urine, didn't you?"

"Something like that!" Marcus shouted, throwing his hands in the air. "Suddenly, I tripped over a stone, and the amphora slipped from my hands. There was a terrible crash!"

"And what happened then?" Severus asked, his expression unchanged. "Didn't the urine just spill onto the ground?"

"I wish that had been the case," Marcus murmured. "But, oh my friends, a wealthy merchant was standing right there—"

"Mercator dives?" Aurelia oculos dilatavit. "Dic mihi, Marcus, num illum inquinavisti?"

"Immo!" Marcus exclamavit, caput inclinans quasi miserandus esset. "Lotium totum in eius togam purpuream effusum est. Effusum, dico!"

Post breve silentium, omnes simul riserunt, excepto Severo, qui tamen labia sua cohibere vix potuit.

"Togam purpuream?" Rufus inter risum dixit. "Pro di immortales, Marcus, ille mercator certe te occidere voluit!"

"Non solum voluit, sed prope fecit," Marcus respondit. "Clamavit: 'Quomodo audes me inquinare?' Et, amici, dominus fullonicae advenit et me coram eo obiurgavit!"

"Ah, misere," Tullia subridens dixit. "Sed dic mihi, quid dixisti domino tuo?"

"Quid potui dicere?" Marcus respondit, umeris elevatis. "Dixi: 'Domine, casu accidit.' Sed ille clamavit: 'Me taedet! Abi! Non te hic amplius volo!' Et sic opus meum perdidi."

Omnes iterum riserunt. Aurelia, quae iam lacrimas risu tenere non poterat, dixit: "Marce, certe tu summam artem habes ad turbas excitandas. Numquam talem historiam in vita mea audivi!"

"Quid? Tu putas hoc esse ridiculum?" Marcus respondit, paulum iratus. "Ego vero miser sum! Nunc pecuniam non habeo, et vos omnes de me ridetis!"

Rufus, adhuc ridens, ad Marcum accessit et manum super humerum eius posuit. "Noli irascere, Marce," inquit. "Ego certe tibi ignosco. Et, si mihi vinum afferes, fortasse etiam aliquid pecuniae mutuabor."

Marcus eum aspiciens respondit: "Ah, Rufe, semper iocos facis! Sed vinum non habeo, nec pecuniam, nec fortunam. Ego sum nihil."

"A wealthy merchant?" Aurelia's eyes widened. "Tell me, Marcus, did you soil him?"

"Indeed!" Marcus exclaimed, bowing his head as if he were the most pitiable man alive. "The entire amphora of urine spilled onto his purple toga. Spilled, I say!"

After a brief silence, everyone burst out laughing—except for Severus, who could barely keep his lips from curling into a smile.

"A purple toga?" Rufus said amidst his laughter. "By the immortal gods, Marcus, that merchant must have wanted to kill you!"

"Not only did he want to, he almost did," Marcus replied. "He shouted, 'How dare you soil me?' And, my friends, the master of the *fullonica* came and scolded me right in front of him!"

"Oh, poor you," Tullia said with a grin. "But tell me, what did you say to your master?"

"What could I say?" Marcus replied, shrugging. "I said, 'Master, it was an accident.' But he shouted, 'I'm fed up! Get out! I don't want you here anymore!' And so I lost my job."

Everyone laughed again. Aurelia, who was now wiping tears from her eyes from laughing so hard, said: "Marcus, you truly have a special talent for causing chaos. I've never heard a story like this in my life!"

"What? You think this is funny?" Marcus replied, slightly annoyed. "I'm truly miserable! Now I have no money, and all of you are laughing at me!"

Rufus, still chuckling, walked over to Marcus and placed a hand on his shoulder. "Don't be angry, Marcus," he said. "I certainly forgive you. And, if you bring me some wine, perhaps I'll even lend you some money."

Marcus, looking at him, replied: "Ah, Rufus, you're always joking! But I have no wine, no money, no fortune. I am nothing."

Severus, qui diu tacuerat, tandem dixit: "Marce, tua culpa fuit, sed simul fortuna te laedit. Nihilominus, melius est ridere de malis quam flere."

"Facile tibi est dicere, Severe," Marcus murmurat. "Tu numquam amphoram lotii portavisti."

"Et pro hoc gratias ago," Severus respondit, subridebat tamen.

Aurelia et Tullia inter se oculos dederunt, deinde Aurelia dixit: "Marcus, nos omnes tibi parcimus, sed modo unum rogo. Num mercator ille adhuc togam purpuream gerit?"

Omnes iterum riserunt. Marcus, cum vultu paulum mollito, tandem subridens respondit: "Ah, ridete, amici, ridete. At memineritis, ego sum qui omnia lotium portavi!"

Clamor risus iterum conclave implevit. Marcus, licet paulum humilitatus, in risum amicorum se iunxit. Et sic nox finem cepit, cum omnes circum mensam sederent, iocis et risu vitam miseri laborantis obliti.

Severus, who had remained silent for a long time, finally said: "Marcus, it was your fault, but at the same time, fortune has been unkind to you. Nevertheless, it is better to laugh at misfortune than to cry over it."

"It's easy for you to say, Severus," Marcus muttered. "You've never had to carry an amphora of urine."

"And for that, I am grateful," Severus replied, though he allowed himself a small smile.

Aurelia and Tullia exchanged glances, and then Aurelia said: "Marcus, we all forgive you, but I just have one question. Is that merchant still wearing his purple toga?"

Everyone burst out laughing again. Marcus, his expression softening slightly, finally managed a small smile and replied: "Ah, laugh, my friends, laugh. But remember, I'm the one who carried all the urine!"

Once more, the room was filled with the sound of laughter. Marcus, though a little humbled, joined in the laughter of his friends. And so the night came to an end, with everyone sitting around the table, forgetting the struggles of a laborer's life with jokes and laughter.

Aurelia et Lucius: Novus Amicus

Aurelia, post longum diem cum amicis suis in insula, sedebat in angulo cubiculi, vultu tristi. Rufus, Severus, et Marcus semper clamabant, ridebant, et de suis miseris laboribus loquebantur. Aurelia suspiravit. "Cur semper cum his tribus stultis tempus perdo?" sibi dixit. "Volo aliquid melius, aliquid splendidum. Forsitan… novum amicum."

Die proximo, dum per vias Carthaginis ambulabat, aureus sol super urbem fulgebat, et odore florentium arborum aer suavis erat. Aurelia, veste simplici induta, tamen oculis micantibus, forum adiit. Multitudinem inter ambulantes vidit virum splendidum, togam albam nitidam gerentem, cum anulo aureo in manu. Vir eam observavit et, subridens, accessit.

"Salve, domina," inquit, voce molli. "Nonne pulchra dies est ad forum visitandum?"

Aurelia, paulum rubescens, respondit: "Salve, domine. Vere, dies est pulcher. Sed… quis es tu?"

Vir risit. "Me Lucium vocant. Mercator sum, sed non semper de divitiis cogito. Saepe quaero… bonos amicos."

"Bonos amicos?" Aurelia subridens respondit. "Dives es, et tamen simpliciter loqueris. Ego sum Aurelia."

"Pulchrum nomen," Lucius dixit, paulum inclinatus. "Sed tu sola ambulas? Nonne amici tui te comitantur?"

"Amici?" Aurelia murmurat, oculos avertens. "Tres pueri sunt… semper pauperes, semper stulti. Ego aliam vitam quaero."

Lucius ad eam propius accessit. "Forsitan ego tibi novam vitam ostendere possum. Mihi concede ut te hodie in foro comiter sim."

Aurelia, vultu laeto, caput annuit. "Non recuso, Luci. Quid proponis?"

Lucius, manu Aureliam leviter tangens, eam ad tabernas opulentas duxit. Taberna prima erat plena vestium delicatarum, purpurae et lanae subtilissimae. "Hic," inquit, "habemus vestes quae te reginam reddent."

Aurelia and Lucius: A New Friend

Aurelia, after a long day with her friends in the apartment, sat in the corner of the room with a sad expression. Rufus, Severus, and Marcus were always shouting, laughing, and complaining about their miserable jobs. Aurelia sighed. "Why do I keep wasting my time with these three fools?" she thought to herself. "I want something better, something grand. Perhaps… a new friend."

The next day, as she walked through the streets of Carthage, the golden sun shone brightly over the city, and the air was sweet with the scent of blooming trees. Dressed in simple attire but with sparkling eyes, Aurelia headed to the forum. Amid the bustling crowd, she noticed a splendid man wearing a bright white toga and a golden ring on his hand. The man noticed her and, smiling, approached.

"Greetings, lady," he said in a soft voice. "Isn't it a beautiful day to visit the forum?"

Aurelia, blushing slightly, replied: "Greetings, sir. Indeed, it is a lovely day. But… who are you?"

The man laughed. "They call me Lucius. I'm a merchant, but I don't always think about wealth. Often, I seek… good friends."

"Good friends?" Aurelia replied with a smile. "You're wealthy, and yet you speak so simply. I am Aurelia."

"A beautiful name," Lucius said, bowing slightly. "But are you walking alone? Don't your friends accompany you?"

"Friends?" Aurelia murmured, averting her eyes. "Three boys… always poor, always foolish. I'm looking for a different life."

Lucius stepped closer to her. "Perhaps I can show you a new life. Allow me to accompany you through the forum today."

Aurelia, her face lighting up, nodded. "I won't refuse, Lucius. What do you suggest?"

Lucius, gently touching Aurelia's hand, led her to luxurious shops. The first shop was filled with exquisite garments, fine purple cloth, and the softest wool. "Here," he said, "we have clothes that will make you a queen."

Aurelia, oculis admirantibus, vestes attigit. "Quam suaves sunt! Sed tales vestes numquam mihi permittere potero."

Lucius, subridens, respondit: "Si reginam videris, fortasse regina eris. Vestes pulchritudinem tuam augent, Aurelia. Noli recusare."

"Reginam?" Aurelia subridens dixit. "Nihil tale umquam habui. Vestes meae… simplices sunt."

"At nunc," Lucius dixit, "vestes tuae erunt tales quae omnium oculos capient." Servum tabernae vocavit et dixit: "Ostende dominae nostrae purpureas tunicas et stolas quas optimas habes."

Aurelia, stupens, purpuream stolam cepit et eam contra corpus suum tenuit. "Lucius," inquit, "sed nimis pretiosa est. Non possum talem stolam emere."

Lucius risit. "Tu nihil emes, Aurelia. Hoc donum meum est. Quid tibi placeat, id accipies."

"Donum tuum?" Aurelia, oculis coruscantibus, quaesivit. "Cur tam generosus es?"

"Quia," Lucius subridens respondit, "pulchritudo tua meretur haec omnia."

Aurelia, vestibus ornata, speculum spectavit et se paene agnovit. "Vide me!" clamavit. "Num ego vera domina sum? Luci, hoc est incredibile."

Lucius manum suam extendit et Aureliae dixit: "Venias mecum, Aurelia. Hic tantum initium est. Cena splendida nos exspectat."

In taberna cenatoria Lucius Aureliam sedere fecit, cibos et vinum deliciae offerens. "Aurelia," inquit, "vita tua, quae nunc tibi dura videtur, potest mutari. Ego adesse possum ut te adiuvem."

Aurelia, iam vino paulum ebriata, respondit: "Luci, tu es vir mirabilis. Mihi videtur fortuna mea tandem melior fieri."

Aurelia, her eyes full of wonder, touched the garments. "How soft they are! But I could never afford such clothes."

Lucius, smiling, replied: "If you look like a queen, perhaps you will become one. These clothes will enhance your beauty, Aurelia. Don't refuse."

"A queen?" Aurelia said with a smile. "I've never had anything like this. My clothes… are simple."

"But now," Lucius said, "your clothes will be the kind that capture everyone's attention." He called the shop attendant and said, "Show our lady your finest purple tunics and stoles."

Aurelia, astonished, took a purple stole and held it against her body. "Lucius," she said, "but it's far too expensive. I can't buy such a stole."

Lucius laughed. "You won't buy anything, Aurelia. This is my gift to you. Whatever pleases you, you shall have."

"Your gift?" Aurelia asked, her eyes sparkling. "Why are you so generous?"

"Because," Lucius replied with a smile, "your beauty deserves all of this."

Dressed in the garments, Aurelia looked into the mirror and hardly recognized herself. "Look at me!" she exclaimed. "Am I truly a lady? Lucius, this is incredible."

Lucius extended his hand and said to Aurelia: "Come with me, Aurelia. This is only the beginning. A splendid dinner awaits us."

At a fine dining establishment, Lucius seated Aurelia and offered her luxurious food and wine. "Aurelia," he said, "your life, which now seems difficult to you, can change. I can be there to help you."

Aurelia, now slightly intoxicated from the wine, replied: "Lucius, you are an extraordinary man. It seems to me that my fortune is finally improving."

Lucius eam aspexit, subridens. "Tandem," inquit, "ego quoque fortunam bonam habeo, cum talis mulier mecum cenet."

Nox leniter procedebat, et Aurelia, novis vestibus ornata et deliciis impleta, se vere reginam putabat. Lucius, eam manu tenens, sub lumine lunae eam domum comitatus est. "Aurelia," susurravit, "hac nocte, sub hoc caelo stellato, nonne sentis vitam tuam iam mutari?"

Aurelia ad eum respexit, oculis micantibus. "Luci," dixit, "forsitan fortuna mea es. Et hac nocte, omnia pulchra videntur."

Lentus subridens, Lucius eam salutavit et abiit, spe plenus ut iterum convenirent. Aurelia diu sub caelo nocturno stetit, cogitans de die incredibili quem modo habuerat.

Lucius looked at her, smiling. "At last," he said, "I too have good fortune, dining with such a woman by my side."

The night gently progressed, and Aurelia, adorned in her new clothes and filled with exquisite delicacies, truly felt like a queen. Lucius, holding her hand, accompanied her home under the moonlight. "Aurelia," he whispered, "tonight, under this starry sky, don't you feel that your life is already changing?"

Aurelia looked up at him, her eyes shining. "Lucius," she said, "perhaps you are my fortune. And tonight, everything seems beautiful."

With a soft smile, Lucius bid her farewell and departed, full of hope that they would meet again. Aurelia stood for a long time under the night sky, reflecting on the incredible day she had just experienced.

Confusio et Reditus Lucii

In angusto conclavi insulae Carthaginis Marcus, Rufus, Severus, Aurelia, et Tullia congregati erant. Sol iam occiderat, et lumen parvae lucernae paulum umbras in parietes proiectabat. Atmosphaera, ut solet inter hos amicos, plena erat tumultus et risuum. Marcus, quem clamoribus Rufus provocabat, in medio cubiculi clamabat.

"Rufe, tu semper dicis te fortem esse," Marcus dixit, digito in Rufum monstrans, "sed omnes sciunt me melius pila ludere!"

"Te?" Rufus risit. "Tu non es fortis, Marce. Tu solum bene... amphoras lotii frangis!"

Omnes subito riserunt. Aurelia manum ad os posuit ut risum cohiberet, sed non potuit. "O Marce," inquit, "tamen, si vinum tam bene effundas quam lotium, forsan dives esses!"

Marcus, vultu rubescente manibus gesticulans, respondit: "Vos omnes contra me estis! Num nemo hic me defendit?"

Tullia, subridens, dixit: "Marce, nos te amamus, sed verum est: tuae stultitiae semper nos delectant."

Clamor subito interruptus est, cum ianua cubiculi crepuit. Lucius, veste splendida et vultu confidenti, in limine apparuit. Aurelia, Lucium videns, oculis coruscantibus ad eum cucurrit. "Luci!" exclamavit. "Cur non dixisti te venire?"

Lucius Aureliae manum leviter tenuit. "Venire volui ut te iterum viderem, Aurelia. Num diem meliorem invenire potui?"

Sed Marcus, qui Lucium vidit, repente palluit. "Tu!" clamavit, ad Lucium digito tremens monstrans. "Mercator ille! Lotium!"

Lucius vultu paulum duro ad Marcum versus est. "Ah, te agnosco," inquit. "Tu es ille puer qui me lotio implevit."

Rufus subito in scamno collapsus risit tam vehementer ut vix respirare posset. "O di immortales!" clamavit. "Hoc fit melius quam omnia!"

Confusion and the Return of Lucius

In the cramped apartment of the Carthaginian insula, Marcus, Rufus, Severus, Aurelia, and Tullia were gathered. The sun had already set, and the dim light of a small oil lamp cast faint shadows on the walls. The atmosphere, as usual among these friends, was full of noise and laughter. Marcus, provoked by Rufus's taunts, was shouting in the middle of the room.

"Rufus, you always claim to be strong," Marcus said, pointing a finger at Rufus, "but everyone knows I'm better at playing ball!"

"You?" Rufus laughed. "You're not strong, Marcus. You're only good at... breaking amphoras of urine!"

Everyone burst out laughing. Aurelia covered her mouth with her hand to stifle her laughter, but she couldn't hold it in. "Oh, Marcus," she said, "still, if you spilled wine as well as you spill urine, perhaps you'd be rich!"

Marcus, his face reddening, gesticulated wildly and replied: "You're all against me! Is there no one here who will defend me?"

Tullia, smiling, said: "Marcus, we love you, but it's true: your foolishness always entertains us."

The commotion was suddenly interrupted when the door to the room creaked open. Lucius, dressed in splendid attire and exuding confidence, appeared in the doorway. Aurelia, seeing Lucius, ran to him with her eyes sparkling. "Lucius!" she exclaimed. "Why didn't you tell me you were coming?"

Lucius gently took Aurelia's hand. "I wanted to come to see you again, Aurelia. Could I have chosen a better day?"

But Marcus, who saw Lucius, suddenly turned pale. "You!" he shouted, pointing a trembling finger at Lucius. "The merchant! The urine!"

Lucius turned toward Marcus with a slightly stern expression. "Ah, I recognize you," he said. "You're the boy who soaked me in urine."

Rufus suddenly collapsed onto the bench, laughing so hard he could barely breathe. "By the immortal gods!" he shouted. "This just keeps getting better!"

"Luci," Aurelia anxie dixit, "hoc verum est? Num tu es ille mercator?"

"Recte dicis, Aurelia," Lucius respondit, oculos in Marcum figens. "Hic est puer, et hic sermo non mihi oblivioni traditus est."

Marcus, paulum retrocedens, mox verba quaerens, balbutivit: "Ego... nesciebam... hoc non mea culpa fuit! Amphora... ipsa fracta est!"

Lucius tamen, vultu in subridens mutato, repente manum suam ad Marcum extendit. "Non cures, Marce," inquit. "Hoc modo facti sumus ambo notissimi in foro! Et nunc tecum bibere possum, non irasci."

Marcus, qui adhuc confundebatur, manum Lucii trepidus accepit. Rufus iterum risit: "Marcus, vinum melius teneto hoc tempore, amabo!"

Severus, qui totam scenam tacitus observaverat, tandem locutus est: "Hoc quidem raro fit. Mercator et fullonis puer amicitiam faciunt. Num vinum celebramus?"

"Vinum celebramus!" Rufus clamavit, exsurgens. "Lucius solvet, nonne?"

Lucius subridens caput inclinavit. "Certissime, amici. Omnes ad tabernam eamus. Hodie Marcus, Aurelia, et tota vestra insula fortunam habent."

Omnes conclave subito relinquentes tumultuose ad tabernam pervenerunt. Vinum effusum est, sermones tumultuosi facti sunt, et Marcus, sicut mos erat, poculum fregit. Lucius risit tam forte ut lacrimas tenere non posset. "Marce," inquit, "tu verus es fabulator vitae. Tuae res semper sunt maximae."

Post plura pocula Rufus clamorose cantare coepit, dum Tullia et Aurelia choros fingere conabantur. Severus, qui poculum suum lente tenebat, tandem risit et dixit: "Hic tumultus, licet absurdus, mihi placet."

"Lucius," Aurelia said anxiously, "is this true? Are you that merchant?"

"You are correct, Aurelia," Lucius replied, fixing his gaze on Marcus. "This is the boy, and that incident has not been forgotten by me."

Marcus, stepping back slightly and fumbling for words, stammered: "I… I didn't know… it wasn't my fault! The amphora… it broke by itself!"

Lucius, however, his expression softening into a smile, suddenly extended his hand toward Marcus. "Don't worry, Marcus," he said. "In this way, we both became famous in the forum! And now I can drink with you, not be angry."

Marcus, still bewildered, nervously shook Lucius's hand. Rufus laughed again: "Marcus, hold the wine better this time, I beg you!"

Severus, who had silently observed the entire scene, finally spoke: "This is indeed rare. A merchant and a fuller's boy making peace. Shall we celebrate with wine?"

"Let's celebrate with wine!" Rufus shouted, standing up. "Lucius will pay, right?"

Lucius, smiling, nodded his head. "Certainly, friends. Let's all go to the tavern. Today, Marcus, Aurelia, and your entire insula are in luck."

All of them left the room at once and noisily made their way to the tavern. Wine was poured, conversations grew rowdy, and Marcus, as usual, broke a cup. Lucius laughed so hard he couldn't hold back his tears. "Marcus," he said, "you are a true storyteller of life. Your adventures are always the greatest."

After several more cups, Rufus began to sing loudly, while Tullia and Aurelia attempted to mimic dances. Severus, holding his cup slowly, finally laughed and said: "This chaos, though ridiculous, pleases me."

Cum nox in mediam processisset, Marcus, iam ebrius, repente clamavit: "Luci, tu es optimus mercator! Non solum vestes pretiosas, sed etiam risum nobiscum habes."

Lucius, aureum poculum levans, dixit: "Et vos, amici, estis optimi tumultuosi! Hac nocte vinum et risus me impleverunt."

Domum redierunt titubantes, cantantes, et, ut semper, tumultuosi. Conclave insulae iterum impletum est risu, et nox finem sumpsit cum Marcus in scamnum collapsus susurravit: "Luci, si vinum effuderis, non ego sum qui tibi irascor."

As the night wore on, Marcus, already drunk, suddenly shouted: "Lucius, you are the best merchant! Not only do you bring fine clothes, but also laughter to share with us."

Lucius, raising his golden cup, replied: "And you, my friends, are the best kind of troublemakers! Tonight, wine and laughter have filled me."

They returned home, stumbling, singing, and, as always, noisy. The apartment was once again filled with laughter, and the night came to an end with Marcus collapsing onto a bench and murmuring: "Lucius, if you spill the wine, I won't be the one getting angry at you."

Verus Vultus Ostenditur

Sol lente occidebat, dum Marcus in angusto vico Carthaginis ambulabat. Aer erat umidus, et lux rubra vespertina vias ornabat. Marcus, qui adhuc vinum noctis praeteritae in capite sentiebat, murmurat: "Vita mea, licet tumultuosa, interdum etiam iocosa est. Lucius, ille dives mercator, tandem mihi ignovit. Fortasse fortuna mea mutatur."

Sed in angulo viae duo viri robusti, vestibus sordidis et vultibus minacibus, eum exspectabant. Cum Marcus eos vidit, paulum titubavit, sed confidens ad eos accessit. "Salvete, amici," inquit, risum fingens. "Num aliquid voluistis?"

Unus ex viris, statura immani, ad Marcum propius venit. "Tu Marcus es, nonne? Fullonis puer qui Lucium offendit?"

Marcus palluit, risu oblitus. "Ego... bene, quod accidit cum Lucio iam praeteriit. Num Lucius adhuc iratus est?"

Vir robustus subridebat, sed sine laetitia. "Lucius non irascitur," inquit, "sed nos iussit ut te salutemus." Subito manus eius graviter Marcum in pectus percussit. Marcus ad terram cecidit, attonitus.

"Quid agitis?" clamavit Marcus, conatus surgere. Sed alter vir eum pedibus percussit, et paulo post uterque eum immaniter verberabat. "Hoc est pro Lucio," vir clamavit, "qui non obliviscitur nec ignoscit."

Marcus in pavimento humi iacebat, vultu sanguinolento et corpore dolente. "Lucius..." murmurat, vix loqui valens. "Ego... nesciebam..." Postquam viri discesserunt, Marcus vix se movens domum redire conatus est. Severus et Rufus eum in angusto vicolo invenerunt, vultibus territis.

"Marce!" Rufus exclamavit, eum sublevans. "Quid accidit? Num latrones te oppugnaverunt?"

"Lucius..." Marcus vix susurravit. "Non... bonus est. Caveatis illum."

The True Face Revealed

The sun was slowly setting as Marcus walked through a narrow street in Carthage. The air was humid, and the red evening light adorned the streets. Marcus, still feeling the effects of the previous night's wine in his head, murmured: "My life, though chaotic, is sometimes amusing. Lucius, that wealthy merchant, finally forgave me. Perhaps my fortune is changing."

But at the corner of the street, two burly men in dirty clothes and with menacing expressions were waiting for him. When Marcus saw them, he hesitated slightly but, trying to appear confident, approached them. "Greetings, friends," he said, forcing a smile. "Did you need something?"

One of the men, tall and imposing, stepped closer to Marcus. "You're Marcus, aren't you? The fuller's boy who offended Lucius?"

Marcus turned pale, his smile forgotten. "I… well, what happened with Lucius is in the past. Surely, he's no longer angry?"

The burly man smirked, but it was a joyless smile. "Lucius isn't angry," he said, "but he sent us to deliver his regards." Suddenly, the man struck Marcus hard in the chest. Marcus fell to the ground, stunned.

"What are you doing?" Marcus cried, trying to get up. But the other man kicked him, and soon both were beating him mercilessly. "This is for Lucius," one of the men shouted, "who never forgets and never forgives."

Marcus lay on the ground, his face bloodied and his body aching. "Lucius…" he murmured, barely able to speak. "I… I didn't know…" After the men left, Marcus, barely able to move, tried to make his way home. Severus and Rufus found him in a narrow alley, their faces filled with alarm.

"Marcus!" Rufus exclaimed, lifting him up. "What happened? Did robbers attack you?"

"Lucius…" Marcus barely whispered. "He's… not good. Beware of him."

Severus, vultu gravi, caput inclinavit. "Lucius? Num mercator ille? Dic nobis omnia, Marce."

Marcus, vix respirans, omnia narrare coepit. Dum loquebatur, Rufus oculos in Severum torsit. "Aurelia!" clamavit. "Si Marcus verum dicit, illa in periculo est. Lucius eam iam in villam suam duxit."

Severus, vultu subitum mutato, statim dixit: "Properemus. Marcus maneat. Nos Aureliam invenire debemus antequam aliquid peius fiat."

Eodem tempore Aurelia cum Lucio in curru eleganti sedebat, dum equi eos ad villam maritimam ferebant. Via praeter litus ducebatur, et aura maris capillos Aureliae leniter movebat. Lucius, vultu placido sed oculis callidis, eam spectabat.

"Aurelia," inquit, "nonne hic locus est ubi somnia tua vera fieri possunt?"

Aurelia, oculis micantibus, subridens respondit: "Luci, hoc pulchritudinem omnem superat. Num dives es sicut rex? Haec villa tam ampla est!"

"Divitiae meae," Lucius respondit, suaviter subridens, "sunt etiam ampliores. Sed tu, Aurelia, pulchrior es quam omnis huius villae gloria."

Aurelia, paulum rubens, eum respexit. "Luci, num vera dicis? Forsitan ego semper credidi me simplicem esse."

"Simplex pulchritudo tua est," Lucius susurravit. "Sed hic locus, Aurelia, potest te dominam reginamque facere."

Cum ad villam pervenissent, servi Aureliam ad atrium duxerunt, ubi triclinium magno splendore ornatum erat. Mensa plena erat cibis delicatis: pavones assi, panis recens, vinum rubrum in poculis aureis effusum.

Severus, his face serious, bowed his head. "Lucius? The merchant? Tell us everything, Marcus."

Marcus, barely breathing, began to recount everything. As he spoke, Rufus turned his eyes toward Severus. "Aurelia!" he shouted. "If Marcus is telling the truth, she's in danger. Lucius has already taken her to his villa."

Severus, his expression suddenly changing, immediately said: "Let's go. Marcus must stay behind. We have to find Aurelia before anything worse happens."

At the same time, Aurelia was sitting with Lucius in an elegant carriage as the horses carried them toward a seaside villa. The road ran along the coast, and the sea breeze gently tousled Aurelia's hair. Lucius, his face calm but his eyes cunning, watched her closely.

"Aurelia," he said, "isn't this the place where your dreams can come true?"

Aurelia, her eyes sparkling, replied with a smile: "Lucius, this surpasses all beauty. Are you as rich as a king? This villa is enormous!"

"My wealth," Lucius said, smiling smoothly, "is even greater. But you, Aurelia, are more beautiful than all the splendor of this villa."

Aurelia, blushing slightly, looked back at him. "Lucius, are you telling the truth? Perhaps I've always thought of myself as simple."

"Your simplicity is your beauty," Lucius whispered. "But this place, Aurelia, can make you a lady and a queen."

When they arrived at the villa, servants escorted Aurelia to the atrium, where the dining room was lavishly decorated. The table was laden with exquisite foods: roasted peacocks, fresh bread, and red wine poured into golden goblets.

"Luci," Aurelia exclamavit, "hoc est nimis! Num semper ita vivis?"

"Hoc est tantum initium," Lucius respondit, manum suam super eius brachium ponens. "Nunc epulemur et gaudeamus. Sed memento, Aurelia, non omnes amici tui hoc merentur."

Aurelia, dum vinum sorbebat, paulum risit. "Amici mei? Marcus, Rufus, Severus? Non intelligunt talem vitam. Sed... quid de eis?"

Lucius vultum serius induit. "Amici tui," inquit, "possunt te trahere retro. Si mecum manes, Aurelia, non potes ad illos redire."

Aurelia, paulum confusa, vinum posuit. "Luci, hoc est durum. Sed—fortasse tu verum dicis. Forsitan alia vita me vocat."

Interea, Rufus et Severus, per vias Carthaginis humidis properantes, tandem ad villam Lucii pervenerunt. Nubes atrae caelum obruerant, venti acriores folia volitabant. Severus vultu gravi dixit: "Villam intrare debemus antequam sero sit."

Post circumeundi conatus, tandem parvum ostium invenerunt. Cum intra villam furtim intravissent, voces sub ianua audierunt. Lucius suaviter loquebatur: "Amici tui non tibi conveniunt, Aurelia. Mecum futura es regina."

Severus dentes strinxit. "Nunc agamus," inquit, "Lucius non scit quid possimus."

"Lucius," Aurelia exclaimed, "this is too much! Do you always live like this?"

"This is only the beginning," Lucius replied, placing his hand gently on her arm. "Now let us feast and enjoy ourselves. But remember, Aurelia, not all of your friends deserve this."

Aurelia, sipping her wine, laughed softly. "My friends? Marcus, Rufus, Severus? They wouldn't understand a life like this. But… what about them?"

Lucius's face grew more serious. "Your friends," he said, "might hold you back. If you stay with me, Aurelia, you cannot return to them."

Aurelia, slightly confused, set her wine down. "Lucius, that's a harsh thing to say. But—perhaps you're right. Maybe another life is calling me."

Meanwhile, Rufus and Severus, hurrying through the damp streets of Carthage, finally reached Lucius's villa. Dark clouds had covered the sky, and sharp winds tossed leaves into the air. Severus, his face grim, said: "We must enter the villa before it's too late."

After searching for a way in, they eventually found a small side door. Once inside, they crept through the villa and heard voices behind a door. Lucius was speaking smoothly: "Your friends are not suited for you, Aurelia. With me, you will be a queen."

Severus clenched his teeth. "We act now," he said. "Lucius doesn't know what we're capable of."

Pugna in Villa Lucii

Noctis silentio, villa Lucii obscurior videbatur quam antea Aureliae visa erat. Atrium, quod primo splendens et magnum apparuerat, nunc magis instar carceris sibi videbatur. Aurelia, stans prope fenestram cubiculi magnifici, animadvertit portas villam circumcludentes firmiter clausas esse. Servi, qui initio videbantur benigni, nunc vultu frigido et vigilantia stricta eam observabant. Lucius, togam leniter gerens, intravit, poculum vini manibus tenens.

"Aurelia," suaviter dixit, "cur tam tacita es? Nonne tibi placet hic locus?"

Aurelia paulum titubavit antequam respondit. "Locus pulcher est," inquit, "sed cur tam solitaria sum? Num amica tua esse non satis est ut libertatem meam retineam?"

Lucius risit, sed subridebat vultu quasi vulpis dolosae. "Libertas, mea Aurelia?" inquit. "Hic, in villa mea, omnia quae desideras habere potes. Libertas autem aliquid est quod fortasse tibi non opus est."

Aurelia paulum retraxit. "Quid hoc significat, Luci?" quaesivit, nunc voce paulo tremens. "Nonne revera amicus meus es?"

Lucius, vinum posuit et propius accessit, manum super humerum eius ponens. "Amicus sum, sed plura tibi dare possum. Regina huic villae esse potes, sed debes meum imperium accipere."

Antequam Aurelia respondere potuit, tumultus in atrio auditus est. Porta magna cum fragore aperta est, et voces altae clamabant. Rufus et Severus, gladios breves tenentes, in atrium irrupuerunt, vultibus firmis et oculis flammantibus.

"Luci!" Rufus clamavit. "Relinque Aureliam! Non sinemus ut eam retineas."

Lucius, primo attonitus, cito se composuit et manum levavit ad servos suos vocandos. "Capite eos!" iussit. Duo servi armati celeriter apparuerunt, gladios suos vibrantes, et Severum ac Rufum adgressi sunt.

The Fight in Lucius's Villa

In the silence of the night, Lucius's villa appeared darker to Aurelia than it had before. The atrium, which had seemed grand and splendid at first, now felt more like a prison. Standing near the window of the magnificent room, Aurelia noticed that the gates surrounding the villa were firmly shut. The servants, who had initially seemed kind, now watched her with cold expressions and strict vigilance. Lucius entered, wearing his toga gracefully and holding a cup of wine.

"Aurelia," he said softly, "why are you so quiet? Don't you like this place?"

Aurelia hesitated slightly before responding. "The place is beautiful," she said, "but why am I so isolated? Is being your companion not enough for me to keep my freedom?"

Lucius laughed, but his smile carried the slyness of a fox. "Freedom, my Aurelia?" he said. "Here, in my villa, you can have everything you desire. But freedom is perhaps something you don't truly need."

Aurelia stepped back slightly. "What does that mean, Lucius?" she asked, her voice now trembling slightly. "Are you not truly my friend?"

Lucius set down his wine and moved closer, placing his hand on her shoulder. "I am your friend, but I can offer you so much more. You can be the queen of this villa, but you must accept my rule."

Before Aurelia could respond, a commotion was heard in the atrium. The large doors burst open with a crash, and loud voices shouted. Rufus and Severus, holding short swords, stormed into the atrium with determined faces and blazing eyes.

"Lucius!" Rufus shouted. "Release Aurelia! We will not let you keep her."

Lucius, startled at first, quickly regained his composure and raised his hand to summon his servants. "Seize them!" he ordered. Two armed servants appeared swiftly, their swords flashing, and charged at Severus and Rufus.

Severus, qui semper in pugnis callidus erat, unum servum scuto repulit, dum Rufus alium gladio proxima pila pulsavit. Clamor et fragor per villam resonabat, dum pugna ferox incipiebat. Aurelia, retrocedens, angulum cubiculi quaerebat, oculis anxiis Lucium spectans. Lucius, paulum trepidus, ad Aureliam se vertit et clamavit: "Si mecum manes, tua vita salva erit. Illi non possunt te servare."

"Non credo tibi," Aurelia respondit, voce plena irae. "Amici mei me vere amant. Tu autem me pro re tua putas!"

Dum Severus unum servum vulneravit et Rufus alium in pavimentum proiecit, Lucius gladium suum ex balteo rapuit. "Audax es, sed hic dies ultimus erit," Lucius clamavit, gladium vibrans. Rufus et Severus parati steterunt, Lucium circumdantes. Aurelia autem, animo firmato, poculum vini, quod Lucius prius posuerat, in faciem eius iecit. Lucius, oculis claudens et iratus, in terram titubavit.

"Curramus!" Severus clamavit, Aureliam manibus trahens. Rufus, procul servos moratus, eos secutus est. Cum per atrium effugerent, pluvia gravis subito cecidit, ventus ululans et fulgura caelum illuminantia.

"Porta illa!" Rufus clamavit, ostium laterale ostendens. "Cito, antequam alii veniant!" Omnes per ostium effugerunt, pedibus madidis et vestibus lotis, sed integri. In via per umbras Carthaginis fugerunt, donec tandem insulam suam attigerunt.

Cum conclave suum ingressi sunt, Marcus et Tullia anxii eos exceperunt. "Quid accidit?" Tullia quaesivit, oculis latronum instar apertis. "Aurelia, bene es?"

"Lucius..." Aurelia susurravit, sed Rufus eam interpellavit. "Lucius non amplius tibi nocebit. Sed periculum adhuc adest. Servi eius nos quaerent."

Severus, dum gladium suum deponit, vultu gravi dixit: "Hic nocte vigilabimus. Si quid mali acciderit, parati erimus."

Severus, always skilled in combat, deflected one servant with his shield, while Rufus struck another against a nearby pillar with his sword. The clash and noise echoed through the villa as the fierce fight began. Aurelia, retreating, sought the corner of the room, her anxious eyes fixed on Lucius. Lucius, slightly shaken, turned to Aurelia and shouted: "If you stay with me, your life will be spared. They cannot save you."

"I don't believe you," Aurelia replied, her voice full of anger. "My friends truly care about me. You only see me as something to possess!"

While Severus wounded one servant and Rufus threw the other to the ground, Lucius drew his sword from his belt. "You are bold, but this will be your last day," Lucius shouted, brandishing his sword. Rufus and Severus stood ready, surrounding Lucius. But Aurelia, her resolve hardening, grabbed the cup of wine Lucius had previously set down and threw it in his face. Lucius, closing his eyes and enraged, stumbled to the ground.

"Let's run!" Severus shouted, grabbing Aurelia by the hand. Rufus, holding back the remaining servants, followed after them. As they fled through the atrium, heavy rain suddenly began to fall, the wind howling and lightning illuminating the sky.

"That door!" Rufus shouted, pointing to a side entrance. "Quickly, before more come!" They all escaped through the door, their feet soaked and their clothes drenched, but unharmed. They ran through the shadows of Carthage's streets until they finally reached their insula.

When they entered their apartment, Marcus and Tullia greeted them anxiously. "What happened?" Tullia asked, her wide eyes resembling those of a thief. "Aurelia, are you okay?"

"Lucius…" Aurelia murmured, but Rufus interrupted her. "Lucius will no longer harm you. But the danger isn't over. His servants will come after us."

Severus, setting down his sword with a serious expression, said: "We will keep watch tonight. If anything happens, we'll be ready."

Aurelia, lacrimas continens, ad Rufum et Severum se vertit. "Gratias vobis ago," inquit, voce tremens. "Me servastis. Numquam hoc obliviscar."

Nox autem, licet plena trepidationis, inter amicos finita est. Omnes, licet fessi et anxii, in conclavi suo tandem quietem invenerunt, scientes se nunc adversus Lucium et eius servos paratos esse.

Aurelia, holding back tears, turned to Rufus and Severus. "Thank you," she said, her voice trembling. "You saved me. I will never forget this."

The night, though filled with unease, ended among friends. All of them, though exhausted and anxious, finally found some rest in their apartment, knowing they were now prepared to face Lucius and his servants if necessary.

Divitiae Inopinatae

Nox illa tumultuosa in villa Lucii non solum amicis periculosa erat, sed etiam magnum secretum latebat. Dum pugna inter Rufum, Severum, et servos Lucii fervebat, unus ex sceleratis, nomine Damas, callide in umbris latens consilium suum faciebat. Vultu anxio sed animo firmo, Damas in horreum ingressus est, ubi aurum et argentum congestum iacebat. Sacculis gravibus, plenis nummorum aureorum et argenteorum, se oneravit et caballum parvum, qui prope stabam, ad fugam paravit.

Interea tumultus pugnae per villam resonabat. Damas, quamvis sagitta in humero vulneratus, manum super vulnus ponens, fortiter equum egit per portas laterales, in tenebras noctis disparens. Lucius, qui tunc Rufum et Severum contra se stantes spectabat, nihil de fuga scelerati suspicatus est.

Equus Damae per vias asperas nocturnas Carthaginis properavit, dum sanguis ex vulnere eius paulatim defluebat. Damas, iam paene exanimis, tandem prope auroram insulam amicorum nostrorum attigit. Severus, qui mane surrexerat ut aquam de via afferret, eum iacentem in via invenit. "Quis es tu?" rogavit Severus, cum curiositate sed etiam cautela.

Damas, paulum susurrans, oculos aperuit. "Ego… ego ex villa Lucii… Fugere conatus sum… Aurum habeo, multum… me absconde…" Haec verba vix dixit, dum sanguis eius in terram effundebatur.

Severus eum sublevavit et in insulam traxit, licet corpus eius iam grave esset. Rufus, qui clamorem Severi audiverat, ad ianuam venit. "Severe! Quid accidit?" Rufus rogavit, dum Severus corpulentum virum in scamno posuit.

"Est ex villa Lucii," Severus dixit, sudore perlatus. "Videtur aurum habere… sed paene mortuus est."

Aurelia et Tullia, quae clamores audiverant, ex cubiculis suis cucurrerunt. Aurelia, oculis latronem intuentibus, dixit: "Quis est hic? Et quid sibi vult hoc aurum?"

Unexpected Riches

That tumultuous night at Lucius's villa was not only perilous for the friends but also held a great secret. While the fight between Rufus, Severus, and Lucius's servants raged on, one of the criminals, named Damas, hid in the shadows, forming his own plan. With an anxious expression but a resolute mind, Damas slipped into the villa's storeroom, where piles of gold and silver were kept. Loading himself with heavy sacks filled with gold and silver coins, he saddled a small horse standing nearby, ready to flee.

Meanwhile, the noise of the fight echoed through the villa. Damas, though wounded in the shoulder by an arrow, pressed his hand against his injury and urged the horse through a side gate, disappearing into the darkness of the night. Lucius, who at that moment was facing Rufus and Severus, remained completely unaware of the criminal's escape.

Damas's horse galloped through the rough, nocturnal streets of Carthage, while blood slowly flowed from his wound. Nearly unconscious, he finally reached the insula of our friends just before dawn. Severus, who had risen early to fetch water from the street, found him lying in the road. "Who are you?" Severus asked, both curious and cautious.

Damas, barely whispering, opened his eyes. "I… I come from Lucius's villa… I tried to escape… I have gold, much of it… hide me…" These words he could barely utter, as his blood seeped into the ground.

Severus lifted him and dragged him into the insula, though the man's body was already heavy with exhaustion. Rufus, hearing Severus's shouts, came to the door. "Severus! What happened?" Rufus asked, as Severus placed the heavy man on a bench.

"He's from Lucius's villa," Severus said, drenched in sweat. "It seems he has gold… but he's nearly dead."

Aurelia and Tullia, hearing the commotion, rushed from their rooms. Aurelia, staring intently at the thief, said: "Who is this man? And what is the meaning of this gold?"

Damas, voce debili, unum ultimum spiritum traxit. "Hoc aurum… non Lucii est amplius… Vobis relinquo… ego… sum… liberatus…" Et cum his verbis, spiritum efflavit.

Silentium breve per conclave cecidit. Tullia, ad sacculos plenae pecuniae spectans, murmuravit: "Divitiae… vere sunt nostrae?"

Marcus, qui nunc ex alia parte cubiculi apparuit, subito exclamavit: "Divitiae nostrae? Aurelia, num possumus togas purpureas et gemmas emere nunc?"

"Tace, Marce," Severus severo vultu respondit. "Haec pecunia potest nobis et felicitatem et periculum afferre. Lucius hoc aurum quaeret, certum est."

Rufus, caput movens, respondit: "Severus recte dicit. Si divitias servare volumus, caveamus. Insula nostra munitio nostra erit."

Omnes circum sacculos congregati sunt, numerum nummorum aspicientes. Aurelia, quae unum nummum aureum in manu tenebat, subridens dixit: "Nunc vere divites sumus. Sed quid faciemus? Num Lucius statim hic appariturus est?"

Marcus, iam excitatus, dixit: "Primum, vinum bonum ememus. Deinde, Aurelia, pro gemmis loquere, si vis!"

Rufus ridens respondit: "Marcus, semper de vino cogitas. Sed Severus recte dicit: debemus cogitare de periculo."

Post breve consilium, amici conclave suum in arcem magnam pecuniae mutaverunt. Aurelia et Tullia pecuniam in ollis absconderunt, dum Marcus et Rufus ostia firmabant. Severus autem, manu mentum sustinens, cogitabat quid de futuro fieri posset.

"Si Lucius veritatem cognoscat," Severus dixit, "omnia amittamus. Sed si diligentes simus, vita nostra melius fiet."

Tullia, oculos in Severum figens, respondit: "Vita melior, Severe? Forsitan, sed semper timebo. Aurum et argentum semper alios attrahunt."

With a feeble voice, Damas drew one last breath. "This gold… is no longer Lucius's… I leave it to you… I… am… free…" And with these words, he exhaled his final breath.

A brief silence fell over the room. Tullia, staring at the sacks filled with money, murmured: "The riches… are truly ours?"

Marcus, who now appeared from the other side of the room, suddenly exclaimed: "Our riches? Aurelia, can we buy purple togas and gems now?"

"Be quiet, Marcus," Severus responded with a stern expression. "This money can bring us both fortune and danger. Lucius will surely come looking for it."

Rufus, nodding his head, replied: "Severus is right. If we want to keep these riches, we must be cautious. Our insula will be our fortress."

They all gathered around the sacks, examining the coins. Aurelia, holding a golden coin in her hand, smiled and said: "Now we are truly rich. But what will we do? Is Lucius going to appear here immediately?"

Marcus, already excited, said: "First, we'll buy good wine. Then, Aurelia, speak of gems if you want!"

Rufus, laughing, replied: "Marcus, you're always thinking about wine. But Severus is right: we need to think about the danger."

After a brief discussion, the friends turned their apartment into a grand fortress for their newfound wealth. Aurelia and Tullia hid the money in pots, while Marcus and Rufus reinforced the doors. Severus, resting his hand on his chin, pondered what the future might hold.

"If Lucius learns the truth," Severus said, "we could lose everything. But if we are careful, our lives could improve."

Tullia, fixing her eyes on Severus, responded: "A better life, Severus? Perhaps, but I will always be afraid. Gold and silver always attract others."

Nox iam appropinquabat cum amici, post longum diem et multas cogitationes, tandem sedebant in circulo. Aurelia, poculum vini in manu tenens, subridens dixit: "Bene, si periculum est, saltem sumus divites. Num non est aliquid quod omnes vellemus?"

Rufus, ridens, poculum suum levavit. "Vere dicis, Aurelia. Vita tumultuosa est, sed nunc etiam splendida."

Marcus, iocans et risum faciens, dixit: "Ego primum tabernam visitabo. Aurelia, veniesne mecum?"

"Tacete, Marce," Aurelia subridens respondit. "Habemus divitias, sed nunc etiam habeamus prudentiam."

Amici, quamvis anxii de periculis futuri, tamen spe et risu vitam novam in insula sua cum pecunia et magnis somniis compleverunt.

The night was approaching as the friends, after a long day of deliberation and many thoughts, finally sat together in a circle. Aurelia, holding a cup of wine in her hand and smiling, said: "Well, if there is danger, at least we are rich. Isn't there something we've all dreamed of?"

Rufus, laughing, raised his cup. "You're right, Aurelia. Life is chaotic, but now it's also dazzling."

Marcus, joking and making everyone laugh, said: "The first thing I'll do is visit a tavern. Aurelia, will you come with me?"

"Be quiet, Marcus," Aurelia responded with a smile. "We have wealth, but now let us also have wisdom."

The friends, though still anxious about the dangers ahead, filled their new life on the insula with hope and laughter, their newfound fortune sparking great dreams for the future.

Fuga Periculosissima

Sol lente oriebatur super Carthaginem, et amici—Rufus, Severus, Marcus, Aurelia, et Tullia—paulum respirabant post tumultuosos eventus noctis. In insula sua sedebant, sacculos plenos pecuniae circum se habentes. Marcus, dum vinum in poculo miscet, risit. "Videte, amici, divites sumus! Nihil nobis timendum est. Lucius certe ne cogitet quidem nos aurum habere."

Aurelia, brachiis super pectus crossis, vultu serio respondit: "Marce, nimis confidens es. Num oblitus es quid Lucius possit facere? Memento, is vir periculosus est."

Severus caput inclinavit. "Aurelia recte dicit. Debemus consilia capere. Ubi abscondemus aurum?"

Rufus, qui prope fenestram sedebat, subito vultu palluit. "Equus! Pro di immortales, obliti sumus equum!"

Omnes statim tacuerunt. Aurelia, oculis dilatatis, murmurat: "Equus? Is adhuc extra insulam est? Nesciebam eum nobis relinquisse!"

Subito clamor ex platea auditus est. Rufus, ex fenestra prospiciens, vidit unum ex viris Lucii, vultu fero et manibus fortibus, prope equum stantem. Vir, equum oculis intuens et vulnus in eius latere animadvertens, subito convertit se et per vias cucurrit.

"Nos deprehensi sumus!" Rufus exclamavit, saltans e sella. "Lucius sciet omnia! Fugere debemus statim!"

Aurelia, trepida, sacculos aureorum manu cepit. "Sed quo fugiemus? Non possumus hic manere!"

"Portemus aurum!" Severus clamavit. "Non possumus hoc relinquere. Marce, cape illam ollam argenteam! Tullia, adi Aureliam cum sacculis!"

Amici statim tumultuose moverunt, sacculos et ollas rapientes. Dum per ostium properabant, Marcus, clamoribus vicinorum excitatus, murmurat: "Hic dies pessimus fit! Numquam quietem habemus!"

A Most Dangerous Escape

The sun was slowly rising over Carthage, and the friends—Rufus, Severus, Marcus, Aurelia, and Tullia—were catching their breath after the tumultuous events of the previous night. They sat together in their insula, surrounded by the sacks of coins. Marcus, pouring wine into his cup, laughed. "Look, friends, we're rich! We have nothing to fear. Surely Lucius would never suspect we have the gold."

Aurelia, crossing her arms over her chest with a serious expression, replied: "Marcus, you're too confident. Have you forgotten what Lucius is capable of? Remember, he is a dangerous man."

Severus nodded. "Aurelia is right. We need to make plans. Where will we hide the gold?"

Rufus, sitting by the window, suddenly turned pale. "The horse! By the gods, we forgot about the horse!"

Everyone immediately fell silent. Aurelia, her eyes wide, murmured: "The horse? It's still outside the insula? I didn't realize it was left behind!"

Suddenly, a shout was heard from the street. Rufus, looking out the window, saw one of Lucius's men—a fierce-looking man with strong hands—standing near the horse. The man, eyeing the horse and noticing the wound on its side, suddenly turned and ran down the street.

"We've been discovered!" Rufus exclaimed, jumping from his seat. "Lucius will know everything! We have to flee immediately!"

Aurelia, panicking, grabbed the sacks of gold. "But where will we go? We can't stay here!"

"Carry the gold!" Severus shouted. "We can't leave it behind. Marcus, grab that silver pot! Tullia, help Aurelia with the sacks!"

The friends moved quickly and chaotically, grabbing sacks and pots. As they hurried out the door, Marcus, startled by the shouting of their neighbors, muttered: "This is turning into the worst day! We never get any peace!"

Cum per vias Carthaginis fugerent, clamor virorum Lucii e longinquo audiebatur. "Capite eos!" unus clamavit, dum vestigia amicarum sequebantur. Aurelia, gravata sacculo argenteo, respiciens vidit viros velociter appropinquantes. "O di immortales, celerius currite! Parum spatii inter nos est!" exclamavit, dum nummi in sacculo graviter resonabant.

Marcus, iam anhelans et sudore madens, cum sacculo magno in manibus, exasperatus clamavit: "Cur ego sacculum gravissimum porto? Rufus, cape hoc! Ego moriar si plus curram!"

Rufus, ridens sed etiam anhelans, respondit: "Tace, Marce, et curre! Lucius te non exspectabit si nos ceperint!"

Amici per forum cucurrerunt, ubi mercatores et venditores eorum clamores audiverunt. "Move, stulte!" Marcus clamavit, dum in mercatorem cum corbe pomorum incedebat. Pomorum corbis subito in terram cadens, pomis ubique volventibus, venditorem ad iram excitavit. "Tu, nebulone! Redde mihi poma!" venditor clamavit, sed Marcus iam fugiebat.

Viri Lucii, gladios vibrantes, eos per turbas sequebantur. Unus ex viris in servum cum amphora plena lotii impetum fecit. Amphora subito fracta est, lotio in omnem partem effuso, et vir clamoribus magna voce imprecatus est: "Malum! Foetor hic me necat!"

Servus, iratus et per lotium madidus, ululans fragmentum amphorae fractae arripuit et virum Lucii minaciter persequi coepit. "Redde mihi amphoram! Redde mihi dignitatem!" clamavit, fragmentum in manu vibrans quasi gladium. Spectatores, risu suffocati, clamores servorum et tumultum spectabant, dum chaos vias implebat et crescit.

Tullia, veste sua paene rupta, clamavit: "Non possumus citius currere! Aurelia, quid facimus?"

As they fled through the streets of Carthage, the shouts of Lucius's men echoed in the distance. "Catch them!" one of the men yelled, their footsteps drawing closer and closer to the fleeing friends. Aurelia, burdened by a sack of silver, glanced back and saw the men rapidly gaining ground. "By the immortal gods, run faster! They're almost upon us!" she exclaimed, the coins in her sack jingling heavily.

Marcus, already panting and drenched in sweat, struggled with a large sack in his hands and cried out in frustration: "Why am *I* carrying the heaviest sack? Rufus, take this! I'll die if I run another step!"

Rufus, laughing but equally breathless, shouted back: "Be quiet, Marcus, and keep running! Lucius won't wait for you if they catch us!"

The friends raced through the marketplace, where merchants and vendors turned to watch the commotion. "Out of the way, fool!" Marcus shouted as he collided with a fruit vendor carrying a basket of apples. The basket tumbled to the ground, apples rolling everywhere, and the enraged vendor yelled, "You scoundrel! Pay for my apples!" But Marcus was already gone.

Lucius's men, brandishing swords, pushed their way through the crowd in pursuit. One of the men crashed into a servant carrying a jar of urine. The jar shattered on impact, and its contents splashed everywhere. The man cursed loudly, shouting, "Damnation! This stench is unbearable!"

The furious servant, drenched and humiliated, grabbed a shard of the broken jar and charged after the man. "Give me back my jar! Return my dignity!" he bellowed, waving the shard like a weapon. Onlookers, doubled over with laughter, watched the chaos unfold as the uproar spread through the streets.

Tullia, her tunic nearly torn from the frenzy, shouted desperately: "We can't run any faster! Aurelia, what do we do?"

Subito, canis parvus, a tumultu excitatus, latrare coepit, dum omnes canem vitare conantes per vias currebant. Canis, latrans et Rufum pedibus mordere conatus, ei obstabat, dum Rufus exclamabat: "Pro di immortales! Ego vinum, non carnem vendo!"

Marcus, videns canem, in plateam lateralem subito detorsit, ubi asinus ligatus prope stabat. Sed asinus, clamores audiens, calcibus aerem feriebat et saccum Marci paene ferit. "O miser asinus!" Marcus clamavit. "Tu peior es quam Lucius ipse!"

Aurelia, animo subito inflammata, sacculum argenteorum cepit. "Hoc eos morabit!" inquit. Subito manum sacculum aperuit, et nummi argentei in aere volitaverunt et cum sonitu in terram ceciderunt.

Populus, cupiditate fulgentibus oculis, subito tumultuose ad nummos properavit. "Argentum!" clamaverunt multi, genua flectentes ut eos colligerent. Unus mercator, qui paulo ante pomis suis sollicitus fuerat, nunc avidus in terram se proiecit clamans: "Haec sunt meliora quam poma!"

Viri Lucii, qui iam prope erant, per turbam prorsus progredi non potuerunt. Unus clamavit: "Apage, stulti! Non pecuniam sed illos quaerimus!" Sed populus eos non audivit. Omnes in terra occupati erant, nummos in manibus avidis colligentes, dum risus et tumultus vias implebant.

Servus, adhuc fragmentum amphorae in manu tenens, unum ex viris Lucii minaciter aspexit. "Si me iterum offenderis, videbis quid potuerim facere!" clamavit, dum ille timidus retrocessit.

Aurelia, videns confusionem, risit, anhelans. "Haec eos impediet! Properemus ad portum!"

Severus caput annuit, manu Tulliam trahens. "Celeriter, amici! Antequam iterum nos sequantur!"

Suddenly, a small dog, startled by the commotion, began barking wildly as everyone dashed through the streets, trying to avoid it. The dog, barking furiously and snapping at Rufus's heels, obstructed his path as Rufus shouted, "By the immortal gods! I sell wine, not meat!"

Marcus, spotting the dog, veered sharply into a side alley, where a tethered donkey stood nearby. However, the donkey, alarmed by the noise, began kicking its legs into the air, nearly striking Marcus's sack. "Oh, miserable donkey!" Marcus exclaimed. "You're worse than Lucius himself!"

Aurelia, suddenly inspired, grabbed her sack of silver. "This will slow them down!" she cried. Without hesitation, she opened the sack and flung the coins into the air. The silver coins sparkled as they scattered, landing on the ground with a resounding clatter.

The townsfolk, their eyes gleaming with greed, surged forward in a frenzy. "Silver!" many shouted, dropping to their knees to collect the coins. One merchant, who had earlier been furious about his spilled apples, now dove eagerly to the ground, exclaiming, "This is far better than apples!"

Lucius's men, who were now closing in, found their path blocked by the chaotic crowd. One of them shouted, "Out of the way, fools! We're after them, not the money!" But the townsfolk ignored him, entirely focused on grabbing as many coins as possible. The street echoed with laughter, shouting, and the clinking of coins as chaos reigned.

Meanwhile, the servant, still clutching the shard of his broken jar, glared menacingly at one of Lucius's men. "If you cross me again, you'll see what I'm capable of!" he yelled, causing the man to retreat cautiously.

Aurelia, watching the confusion unfold, laughed breathlessly. "That should hold them off! Let's head to the port!"

Severus nodded, pulling Tullia by the hand. "Quickly, friends! Before they catch up again!"

Amici, nunc paulo tutiores, per vias portus cucurrerunt. Mare prope fulgebat, ventus marinus capillos eorum movebat. Rufus, sudore perlatus, manus ad navem prope stantem extendit. "Hic! Hoc est nostrum salutis consilium!"

Navis, parva sed firma, stabat in portu, nautae circa eam laborantes. Marcus, adhuc anhelans, in navem prosiluit. "Num ad Siciliam itis? Vel Africam? Tantum ab Lucio nos auferte!"

Nauta, vultu miranti, respondit: "Quid accidit? Cur tam trepidi estis?"

Aurelia, adhuc sacculum argenteorum in manu tenens, firmiter dixit: "Non quaeras. Nos duc per mare. Divitias nostras tibi paulo offeremus."

Nauta, oculis micantibus, caput annuit. "Sic, si pretium bonum offeratis, vos portabo. Sed properate, nam tempestas appropinquat."

Cum amici in navem ascenderunt et ventus vela implevit, mare leniter undabat. Aurelia, in prora stans, subridens dixit: "Forsitan nunc nova vita incipiat. Sed semper timebo Lucium."

Severus, e vicino stans, firmiter respondit: "Nos amicitia nostra servabit. Divitiae sunt periculosissimae, sed simul sunt nostra spes."

Navis paulatim portum reliquit, dum Carthago paene sub stellis nocturnis evanescebat. Amici, fatigati sed simul spe plena, in noctem ignotam navigabant.

As the friends, now slightly safer, ran through the streets of the port, the sea shimmered nearby, and the ocean breeze tousled their hair. Rufus, drenched in sweat, pointed toward a small ship moored close by. "There! That's our escape plan!"

The ship, small but sturdy, rested in the harbor, with sailors bustling around it. Marcus, still panting, leapt aboard. "Are you headed to Sicily? Or Africa? Just take us far away from Lucius!"

A sailor, looking bewildered, paused in his work and asked, "What's happened? Why are you all in such a rush?"

Aurelia, still clutching the sack of silver tightly, answered with determination, "Don't ask questions. Just take us across the sea. We'll make it worth your while."

The sailor's eyes gleamed with interest as he nodded. "Very well, if you pay me handsomely, I'll take you. But hurry—there's a storm approaching."

The friends clambered aboard as the wind began to fill the sails, causing the ship to sway gently. Aurelia, standing at the prow, gazed out toward the open sea and smiled faintly. "Perhaps a new life begins now. But I'll always fear Lucius."

Severus, standing close beside her, replied firmly, "Our friendship will protect us. Wealth may be dangerous, but it's also our hope."

As the ship slowly departed the harbor, the lights of Carthage began to fade beneath the night sky filled with stars. The friends, exhausted but hopeful, sailed into the unknown, ready to face whatever lay ahead.

Amici in Melita

Navis parva, vento et undis leviter mota, tandem ad portum Melitae pervenit. Sol super insulam fulgebat, et aer calidus et dulcis per nares fluebat. Aurelia, in prora navis stans, oculis micantibus portum spectavit. "Videte, amici," clamavit. "Nova vita nos exspectat! Quam pulchra haec insula est!"

Rufus, poculum vini in manu tenens, risit. "Si insula pulchra est, vinum etiam erit bonum. Num hic possumus tranquilli esse et Lucium oblivisci?"

Marcus, sacculum nummorum aureorum in manu tenens, respondit: "Ego non de Lucio cogito. Ego de villa cogito. Nonne dives essem, si meam villam haberem cum atrio amplo et piscinis?"

Tullia, vento capillos eius movente, subridens dixit: "Marcus, num villa te beatum faciet? Semper tu de rebus magnis somnias."

"Somnia magna sunt bona!" Marcus respondit, humeros tollens. "Et nunc habeo aurum ad mea somnia complenda!"

Cum navis portum attigisset, nauta eos exclamavit: "Ad terram, amici! Divitiae vestrae vos exspectant!" Amici, cum saccis pecuniae, celeriter navem reliquerunt et in portum descenderunt. Rufus, qui semper oculos aperte tenebat, tabernas vinarias prope vidit et murmurat: "Nunc, ubi invenire possumus villam et vinum simul?"

Severus, qui post omnes ambulabat et pecuniam suam in sacculo parvo tenebat, vultu serio respondit: "Amici, antequam vinum et villas quaeramus, debemus divitias nostras aeque dividere. Nonne hoc iustum est?"

"Recte dicis, Severe," Aurelia dixit, sacculum argenteorum tenens. "Dividamus omnia. Sed primo loca quieta inveniamus."

Sub umbra magnae arboris sederunt, et Severus saccos aperuit, nummos aureos et argenteos in terram effundens. "Vide, quantus thesaurus est hic!" Tullia exclamavit, oculis coruscantibus. "Num verum est?"

Friends in Malta

The small ship, lightly moved by the wind and waves, finally reached the port of Malta. The sun shone brightly over the island, and warm, sweet air flowed through their noses. Aurelia, standing at the prow of the ship, gazed at the port with sparkling eyes. "Look, friends," she exclaimed. "A new life awaits us! How beautiful this island is!"

Rufus, holding a cup of wine in his hand, laughed. "If the island is beautiful, the wine will surely be good too. Can we finally live peacefully here and forget Lucius?"

Marcus, holding a sack of gold coins in his hand, replied, "I'm not thinking about Lucius. I'm thinking about a villa. Wouldn't I be rich if I had my own villa with a grand courtyard and pools?"

Tullia, her hair blown by the wind, smiled and said, "Marcus, will a villa make you happy? You always dream of great things."

"Big dreams are good!" Marcus replied, shrugging his shoulders. "And now I have the gold to make my dreams come true!"

When the ship reached the port, the sailor shouted to them, "To shore, friends! Your riches await you!" The friends, carrying their bags of money, quickly left the ship and stepped into the port. Rufus, always keeping his eyes wide open, spotted nearby wine shops and murmured, "Now, where can we find a villa and wine together?"

Severus, walking behind everyone and carrying his money in a small pouch, replied seriously, "Friends, before we look for wine and villas, we should divide our riches fairly. Isn't that the right thing to do?"

"You're right, Severus," Aurelia said, holding her sack of silver coins. "Let's divide everything. But first, let's find a quiet place."

They sat under the shade of a large tree, and Severus opened the bags, spilling gold and silver coins onto the ground. "Look at this, what a treasure!" Tullia exclaimed, her eyes gleaming. "Is it real?"

"Tot nummi!" Marcus exclamavit, manibus avidis. "Non putabam me umquam talia videre!"

"Sed memineritis," Severus graviter dixit, "hoc divitias et pericula simul portat. Dividamus nunc aequaliter."

Nummos in quinque partes aequas diviserunt. Aurelia, saccum suum complens, subridens dixit: "Ego villam parvam inveniam, ubi hortum habere possim et rosas colere."

"Et ego," Tullia dixit, "villam cum atrio amplo quaeram, ubi convivium cum amicis habeamus."

Rufus risit et dixit: "Si convivium habes, ego vinum adferam. Villa mea erit prope tuam, Tullia, ut semper bibamus simul."

Marcus, saccum plenum nummorum tenens, clamavit: "Villa mea erit maxima omnium! Hortos, piscinas, et columnas marmoreas habebit. Non possum exspectare!"

Severus, qui partem suam accepit, solum et tacitus mansit. Aurelia eum observans, quaesivit: "Severe, quid facies? Num villam quaeres?"

Severus humeros levavit. "Nescio. Pecuniam habeo, sed quid faciam, nondum certus sum. Num ego villam habeam, cum solum tranquillitatem quaeram?"

Rufus eum in dorsum percussit et risit. "Severe, semper serius es. Etsi villam non vis, venias nobiscum convivium habere!"

Amici per vias Melitae ambulaverunt, villas spectantes et mercatores cum vinis et cibis colloquentes. Marcus et Aurelia tandem parvam villam invenerunt prope litus, cum hortis pulchris et fenestris apertis ad mare. "Hic vivemus," Aurelia dixit, subridens. "Nos reges Melitae erimus!"

Marcus risit et, ad Aureliam se inclinans, respondit: "Et nos convivia splendida habebimus, cum vinis et amicis!"

"So many coins!" Marcus exclaimed, his hands eagerly grasping. "I never thought I would ever see such wealth!"

"But remember," Severus said gravely, "this brings both riches and dangers. Let's divide it equally now."

They divided the coins into five equal parts. Aurelia, filling her sack with a smile, said, "I will find a small villa where I can have a garden and grow roses."

"And I," Tullia added, "will look for a villa with a grand courtyard where we can host feasts with friends."

Rufus laughed and said, "If you host a feast, I'll bring the wine. My villa will be near yours, Tullia, so we can always drink together."

Marcus, holding his sack full of coins, shouted, "My villa will be the largest of all! It will have gardens, pools, and marble columns. I can't wait!"

Severus, who had taken his share, remained silent and thoughtful. Observing him, Aurelia asked, "Severus, what will you do? Are you going to look for a villa?"

Severus shrugged. "I don't know. I have the money, but I'm not sure what to do with it yet. Should I have a villa when all I seek is peace?"

Rufus slapped him on the back and laughed. "Severus, you're always so serious. Even if you don't want a villa, come celebrate with us!"

The friends walked through the streets of Malta, looking at villas and chatting with merchants selling wine and food. Marcus and Aurelia finally found a small villa near the coast, with beautiful gardens and windows that opened to the sea. "We'll live here," Aurelia said, smiling. "We'll be the rulers of Malta!"

Marcus laughed and, leaning toward Aurelia, replied, "And we'll host magnificent feasts, with wine and friends!"

Rufus et Tullia, interea, villam maiorem cum vineis invenerunt. Rufus, folia vinearum manibus tangens, subridens dixit: "Hic locus est! Vinum Melitae optimum fiet nostrum."

Tullia, fenestram villae aperiens et auram marinam sentiens, respondit: "Ego quoque hic beatam me sentio. Hortum hic habebo, et domus nostra semper plena erit laetitia."

Post longum diem villas spectandi et mercatoribus colloquendi, amici in domibus suis se collocaverunt. Marcus et Aurelia in atrio villae suae sedebant, columnas simplices sed elegantes admirantes. Marcus, vinum in poculum fundens, dixit: "Hoc est! Nihil me impedit. Nos vitam nostram hic plenam habebimus."

Rufus et Tullia in vineis suis ambulabant, de futuro suo colloquentes. "Vinum nostrum celebre fiet," Rufus dixit, spe plenus.
"Et villa nostra semper plena erit amicis," Tullia addidit, manum in bracchium Rufum ponens.

Severus autem, solus in via, ad lunam spectabat. Pecuniam suam in sacculo tenens, per vias Melitae vagabatur, villas amicarum et amicorum in longinquo videns. Sed ipse non intravit. Sub umbra arboris magnae sedit, nummos suos intuens.

"Divitiae," Severus murmurat, "sed quid prodest pecunia sine scopo? Aurelia et Tullia nunc reginae sunt, Marcus et Rufus sibi novas vitas incipiunt. Ego autem... quid faciam?"

Nox descenderat, et stellae super insulam Melitam micabant. Severus tamen ibi sedebat, cum pecunia sua, sed sine consilio. Solitudinem et silentium paulatim sentiebat, dum amici eius in villis suis ridebant et novas vitas colebant. Finis huius noctis non Severum implevit spe, sed dubitatione. In umbra et silentio mansit, non sciens quid futurum esset aut quid sibi facere deberet.

Meanwhile, Rufus and Tullia found a larger villa with vineyards. Rufus, running his hands over the vine leaves, smiled and said, "This is the place! The finest wine in Malta will be ours."

Tullia, opening the villa's window and feeling the sea breeze, replied, "I also feel happy here. I'll have a garden, and our home will always be filled with joy."

After a long day of viewing villas and talking to merchants, the friends settled into their new homes. Marcus and Aurelia sat in the courtyard of their villa, admiring the simple yet elegant columns. Marcus, pouring wine into his cup, said, "This is it! Nothing holds me back. We will have a full life here."

Rufus and Tullia walked through their vineyards, discussing their future. "Our wine will become famous," Rufus said, full of hope.

"And our villa will always be filled with friends," Tullia added, placing her hand on Rufus's arm.

Severus, however, was alone, gazing at the moon. Holding his money in a small bag, he wandered the streets of Malta, seeing the distant villas of his friends. But he did not enter. Instead, he sat beneath a large tree, looking at his coins.

"Wealth," Severus murmured, "but what is the point of money without purpose? Aurelia and Tullia are queens now, and Marcus and Rufus are starting new lives. But I... what will I do?"

Night fell, and the stars sparkled over the island of Malta. Yet Severus remained seated there, alone with his money but without a plan. He gradually felt the solitude and silence, while his friends laughed and embraced their new lives in their villas. The end of this night brought Severus no hope, only uncertainty. He stayed in the shadows and silence, not knowing what the future held or what he should do.

Vita Nova et Severi Negotium

Aurelia et Marcus vitam suam in villa prope litus fruebantur. In horto rosas colligere solebant, dum Marcus semper de convivio quod pro amicis parare volebat cogitabat. "Aurelia," clamavit, dum in atrio marmoreo sedebat, "puto me vinum optimum pro convivio invenisse! Nonne illi amici nostri nos laudabunt?"

Aurelia, ridens, dum flores in corbem posuit, respondit: "Marcus, semper de convivio cogitas. Tamen, confiteor, convivium tuum erit magnificum si vinum optimum adferes."

Eodem tempore, Rufus et Tullia in villa prope vineas vivebant. Rufus quotidie vineas suas curabat, dum Tullia novas stolas sibi emere solebat ex pecunia quam nunc amplam habebant. "Rufe," Tullia dixit, spectans novam stolam purpuream, "quid censes de hac veste? Nonne decet me?"

Rufus, poculum vini in manibus, risit et respondit: "Tullia, tu decora es in omni veste. Sed memento, non potes pecuniam tuam omnibus tabernariis dare!"

Interim, Severus, qui solus manebat et pecuniam suam in sacculo servabat, novum consilium cepit. "Nolo pecuniam meam in otio perdere," secum cogitavit. "Melior est vita operosa quam desidiosa." Cum haec dixisset, ad portum Melitae ambulavit, ubi naves Romanae et Graecae mercimonia portabant.

In portu Severus tabernam parvam invenit prope aquam. Taberna vetus erat, sed satis ampla ad mercaturas tractandas. "Hic locus perfectus est," sibi dixit. "Ex hac taberna ego mercator fieri potero."

Postquam tabernam emit, Severus coepit cogitare quid vendere posset. Portus Melitae erat locus ubi multa mercimonia inter Europam, Africam, et Asiam transibant. "Si naviculam meam implevero vino, oleo, et tritico," Severus secum dixit, "haec omnia in urbes maiores Romanae vendere potero. Item, mel et cera ex Sicilia hic bene venire poterunt."

A New Life and Severus' Business

Aurelia and Marcus were enjoying their life in their villa near the coast. They often spent their mornings picking roses in the garden, while Marcus constantly thought about the feast he wanted to host for their friends. "Aurelia," he called out as he lounged in their marble courtyard, "I think I've found the finest wine for our banquet! Won't our friends praise us for it?"

Aurelia, laughing as she placed flowers in a basket, replied, "Marcus, you always think about banquets. But I admit, your feast will be magnificent if you bring the best wine."

Meanwhile, Rufus and Tullia were living in their villa near the vineyards. Rufus tended to his vines daily, while Tullia regularly bought herself new dresses with the wealth they now enjoyed. "Rufus," Tullia said, admiring a new purple gown, "what do you think of this dress? Doesn't it suit me?"

Rufus, holding a cup of wine, chuckled and replied, "Tullia, you look beautiful in any dress. But remember, you can't give all your money to the shopkeepers!"

At the same time, Severus, who had remained alone and kept his money in a pouch, came up with a new plan. "I don't want to waste my wealth on idleness," he thought to himself. "A life of work is better than a life of leisure." Resolving to act, he walked to the port of Malta, where Roman and Greek ships brought their goods.

At the port, Severus discovered a small shop near the water. The shop was old but spacious enough for conducting trade. "This is the perfect spot," he told himself. "From this shop, I can become a merchant."

After purchasing the shop, Severus began planning what he could sell. The port of Malta was a hub for goods traveling between Europe, Africa, and Asia. "If I can fill my small ship with wine, oil, and grain," Severus thought, "I can sell it all in the major Roman cities. Likewise, honey and wax from Sicily will sell well here."

Die postero Severus ad nautas in portu accessit. "Quis vestrum me adiuvare potest in mercatura?" quaesivit. Unus nauta, vultu callido, eum aspexit. "Ego navem habeo, domine," dixit. "Si merces tuas portare vis, te adiuvabo. Sed pretium meum altum erit."

Severus risit. "Altum, dicis? Negotiamur, amice. Ego mercator sum, non stultus." Post longam disputationem, Severus pretium iustum obtinuit et cum nautis foedus fecit. "Incipiam cum vino et oleo," dixit. "Haec merces semper quaeruntur."

Post paucos dies, Severus tabernam suam aperuit. Clientes cito ad eum venerunt, spectantes amphoras vini et olei quae prope portum positae erant. Unus mercator ex Hispania, vultu laeto, dixit: "Hoc vinum optimum videtur! Quid pretium est?"

Severus subridens respondit: "Amphora vini Melitensis tibi constabit quinque denarios. Sed si plures amphoras emes, pretium minuam."

Mercator, paulum cogitans, dixit: "Quinque amphoras mihi vende." Severus pecuniam accepit et amphoras tradidit. "Optime," dixit, "te iterum exspecto. Si vinum tibi placet, semper plus habebo."

Cum nocte domum redisset, Severus in atrio parvo sedebat et pecuniam numerabat. "Haec pecunia melius mihi prodest quam otium," sibi dixit. "Vita mercatoris difficilis est, sed etiam fructuosa."

Interim, Marcus et Aurelia convivia in villa sua celebrabant, dum Rufus et Tullia, vinum ex vineis suis parvum tantum conficientes, quodammodo ad parvas expensas amicis et vicinis vendebant. Severus autem, qui nunc non solum pecuniam, sed etiam novos clientes habebat, paulatim vitam suam implere sentiebat. Sed, cum luna super Melitam splendebat, Severus, solus in taberna sua, iterum secum cogitavit: "Divitiae sunt bonae, sed amicitia melior est. Spero fore ut iterum omnes amici in eodem loco conveniamus."

The following day, Severus approached the sailors at the port. "Who among you can help me with trade?" he asked. One sailor, with a cunning look, glanced at him. "I have a ship, sir," he said. "If you want your goods transported, I'll help you. But my price will be high."

Severus laughed. "High, you say? Let's negotiate, my friend. I'm a merchant, not a fool." After a lengthy discussion, Severus secured a fair price and made a deal with the sailors. "I'll start with wine and oil," he said. "These goods are always in demand."

A few days later, Severus opened his shop. Customers quickly arrived, drawn by the amphoras of wine and oil displayed near the port. One merchant from Spain, with a cheerful expression, said, "This wine looks excellent! What's the price?"

Smiling, Severus replied, "A jar of Melitese wine will cost you five denarii. But if you buy more, I'll lower the price."

The merchant, thinking for a moment, said, "Sell me five jars." Severus accepted the payment and handed over the amphoras. "Excellent," he said, "I'll look forward to your return. If you like the wine, I'll always have more."

When Severus returned home that evening, he sat in his small courtyard, counting his money. "This money serves me better than idleness," he told himself. "The life of a merchant is hard, but it's also rewarding."

Meanwhile, Marcus and Aurelia were hosting feasts in their villa, while Rufus and Tullia, producing only a modest amount of wine from their vineyards, sold it at small prices to friends and neighbors. Severus, however, who now had not only money but also a growing clientele, began to feel his life taking shape.

Yet, as the moon shone brightly over Malta, Severus, sitting alone in his shop, reflected once again: "Wealth is good, but friendship is better. I hope that one day, all of us friends will gather together in the same place again."

Fortuna

Severus, qui vitam operosam egerat, post unum annum Melitae mercatorum locupletissimus factus erat. Taberna eius in portu, ubi vinum, oleum, mel, et cerae venibant, semper plena erat clientibus ex omnibus partibus Imperii Romani. Naves eius mercaturas inter Africam, Italiam, et Siciliam portabant, et pecunia eius paulatim crescebat. "Fortuna mihi favet," Severus secum dixit, numerans denarios aureos in mensa tabernae suae. "Sed, ut semper, labor est radix omnium rerum bonarum."

Interea, Aurelia et Marcus, Rufus et Tullia in villis suis vitam satis otiosam ducebant. Convivia celebrabant, vinum bibebant, et paucos labores suscipiebant. Sed pecunia, licet multa initio, paulatim minuere coepit. Aurelia, in atrio villae sedens et manum super ventrem suum ponens, suspiravit. "Marce," inquit, "ego paulo anxia sum. Nummi nostri fere consumpti sunt."

Marcus, poculum vini exspectans, subridens respondit: "Non cures, mea Aurelia. Fortuna iterum nos adiuvabit."

"Fortuna?" Aurelia vultu severo respondit. "Marce, pecunia e caelo non cadit. Ego nunc de infante nostro cogito. Non possumus sic vivere."

In altera villa, Rufus et Tullia similia verba inter se habebant. Tullia, quae stolam suam inspexit, dixit: "Rufe, ego etiam nunc parvulum exspecto. Sed pecunia nostra paene nulla est. Quid faciemus?"

Rufus, qui semper ad vinum et convivium inclinabat, paulum confusus respondit: "Tullia, fortasse laborare debemus. Sed quid possumus agere? Ego numquam panem coxi aut tabernam rexi."

"Sed nunc est tempus discendi," Tullia respondit, manu super mensam posita. "Si Severus tam dives fieri potuit, num nos non possumus aliquid simile facere?"

Fortune

Severus, who had led a life of hard work, had, after one year, become the wealthiest merchant in Malta. His shop at the port, where he sold wine, oil, honey, and wax, was always crowded with clients from all parts of the Roman Empire. His ships transported goods between Africa, Italy, and Sicily, and his wealth steadily increased. "Fortune favors me," Severus said to himself, counting the gold coins on the table in his shop. "But, as always, hard work is the root of all good things."

Meanwhile, Aurelia and Marcus, Rufus and Tullia lived relatively idle lives in their villas. They hosted feasts, drank wine, and took on few responsibilities. Yet their money, though plentiful at first, began to dwindle. Aurelia, sitting in the courtyard of her villa and placing a hand on her stomach, sighed. "Marcus," she said, "I'm a little anxious. Our coins are almost gone."

Marcus, waiting for his cup of wine, replied with a smile: "Don't worry, my Aurelia. Fortune will help us again."

"Fortune?" Aurelia replied with a stern look. "Marcus, money doesn't fall from the sky. I'm thinking about our baby now. We can't live like this anymore."

In the other villa, Rufus and Tullia were having a similar conversation. Tullia, examining her gown, said, "Rufus, I too am now expecting a little one. But our money is almost gone. What will we do?"

Rufus, who had always leaned towards wine and revelry, responded somewhat sheepishly: "Tullia, perhaps we should work. But what can we do? I've never baked bread or managed a shop."

"But now is the time to learn," Tullia replied, placing her hand firmly on the table. "If Severus could become so wealthy, can't we also do something similar?"

Post longam consultationem, Marcus et Rufus decreverunt se in foro laborare quaesituros esse. Aurelia et Tullia, graviditate fatigatae, domi manserunt, sed spem in viris suis posuerunt.

In foro, Marcus et Rufus multas tabernas visitaverunt, sed nullus eos primo accepit. Tandem, Marcus vidit pistrinum parvum ubi pistrix panem calidum ex fornace educebat. Marcus ad eam accessit et dixit: "Salve, domina. Num opus est tibi adiutor?"

Pistrix, vultu curiosa, Marcum spectavit. "Numquam pistrinum administravisti, nonne?" rogavit.

"Non, sed discere possum," Marcus respondit, vultu fiducioso. "Operam dare paratus sum, etiam si pistrinum meum domum non habeo."

Pistrix risit et annuit. "Bene, veni cras mane. Multum panem coquere debemus."

Interim, Rufus in cauponam prope forum intravit. Dominus cauponae, vultu gravi, eum intuitus est. "Quid vis?" rogavit.

"Operam dare paratus sum," Rufus respondit. "Ego bene vinum effundere possum et clientes servire."

Dominus eum probavit et, subridens, respondit: "Bene. Mane adesto. Sed scito, si vinum effuderis, te dimittam!"

Marcus et Rufus, nunc laboribus inventis, laeti domum redierunt. "Tullia," Rufus clamavit, "ego nunc caupo sum! Non amplius pecuniam tuam timeas."

"Et ego," Marcus Aureliae dixit, "panem cocturus sum! Mox nummos habebimus ut vitam nostram sustineamus."

Quod autem amici nostri non sciebant erat quod pistrinum et caupona ambo Severi erant. Severus, cum laboribus suis occupatus, tamen oculos suos semper in amicis suis habebat. Cum tabernarii eum de novo pistrino et caupo certiorem facerent, subridens dixit: "Bene, amici mei tandem laborare coeperunt. Sed non eis dicam me esse dominum. Tempus est ut ipsi discant quid sit labor."

After a long discussion, Marcus and Rufus decided to look for work in the marketplace. Aurelia and Tullia, fatigued by their pregnancies, stayed home but placed their hopes in their husbands.

In the marketplace, Marcus and Rufus visited many shops, but none hired them at first. Finally, Marcus spotted a small bakery where a baker was pulling warm bread from the oven. Marcus approached her and said, "Greetings, madam. Do you need an assistant?"

The baker, looking at Marcus with curiosity, replied, "You've never worked in a bakery before, have you?"

"No, but I can learn," Marcus answered confidently. "I'm ready to work, even if I don't own a bakery of my own."

The baker laughed and nodded. "Very well, come tomorrow morning. We have a lot of bread to bake."

Meanwhile, Rufus entered a tavern near the forum. The tavern owner, with a serious expression, looked him over. "What do you want?" he asked.

"I'm ready to work," Rufus replied. "I can pour wine well and serve customers."

The owner scrutinized him and, with a slight smile, replied, "Fine. Be here in the morning. But know this: if you spill the wine, you're fired!"

Marcus and Rufus, now having secured jobs, happily returned home. "Tullia," Rufus shouted, "I'm now a tavern keeper! You no longer need to worry about our money."

"And I," Marcus said to Aurelia, "will be baking bread! Soon we'll have the coins we need to sustain our lives."

What the friends didn't know, however, was that both the bakery and the tavern belonged to Severus. Severus, busy with his own enterprises, always kept an eye on his friends. When the shopkeepers informed him of the new baker and tavern keeper, he smiled and said, "Well, my friends have finally started working. But I won't tell them I'm the owner. It's time they learned the value of hard work themselves."

Et sic Marcus et Rufus in novis laboribus suis, diebus mane surgentes, laborem incipiebant. Aurelia et Tullia, gravida et spe plena, domi eos exspectabant. Severus autem, divitiis crescentibus et amicis quasi in umbra adiutis, rursus in tabernam suam rediit, vultu pleno laetitiae. Nova vita amicis Melitae semper nova et plena casuum erat.

And so, Marcus and Rufus began their new jobs, rising early each day to start their work. Aurelia and Tullia, pregnant and full of hope, waited for them at home. Meanwhile, Severus, with his growing wealth and quietly supporting his friends from the shadows, returned to his shop, his face filled with joy. The new life for the friends in Melita remained ever fresh and full of adventures.

Severus Rex Mercatorum

Solis radiis fulgentibus super portum Melitae, Severus in taberna sua magnificenti sedebat, mensam marmoream ante se habens. Aurei et argentei nummi in ordine perfecto iacebant, et Severus eos lente numerabat, subridens sibi. "O fortuna," inquit, "Marcus et Rufus, qui tam diu mecum vitam tumultuosam duxerunt, nunc pro me laborant nec sciunt. Quam dulce est!"

Dum Severus haec verba cogitabat, subito ianua tabernae cum fragore aperta est. Marcus et Rufus, sudore perlati et farina pleni, intraverunt. Marcus tunicam pulvere panis albam habebat, dum Rufus vinum olens vestem paene rubram guttis vinarii maculatam gerebat. Uterque vultu fessissimo sed irato Severum adspiciebat.

"Severe!" Marcus clamavit, manibus gesticulans. "Panem coquere? Quis umquam tam difficilem laborem fecit? Ego plus laboro quam Romulus urbem condidit!"

Rufus, manus in lateribus posuit et subridens respondit: "Tu panem coquens? Ego vinum effundo, clientes iratos paco, et calices frangendos teneo. Tu solum farinam tangis, Marce. Ego vere laboro!"

"Et tu, Rufe," Marcus respondit, "totum diem vinum bibis et de labore quereris. Dii te ament!"

"Tacete, ambo," Severus interposuit, vultu composito sed intus ridens. "Cur tam fessi estis? Dominus vester tam durus videtur?"

"Durus?" Rufus fremuit. "Dominus est peior quam canis rabidus! Nonne potest mihi pecuniam maiorem solvere?"

"Et mihi quoque!" Marcus clamavit. "Panis pretium crescit, sed ego semper eadem pecunia laboro!"

Severus, paulum inclinatus, vultu graviter fingens, respondit: "Eheu, amici, dominus vester certe difficilis est. Sed quid, si vos rogaverit ut plus laboretis?"

Marcus, paulum trepidus, exclamavit: "Plus laborare? Noli iocari, Severe! Ego iam totum diem laboro! Dominus insanit!"

Severus the Merchant King

Under the shining rays of the sun over the port of Melita, Severus sat in his splendid shop, a marble table in front of him. Golden and silver coins lay in perfect order, and Severus counted them slowly, smiling to himself. "Oh, fortune," he said, "Marcus and Rufus, who have led such a chaotic life with me for so long, now work for me and don't even know it. How sweet it is!"

While Severus was musing over these thoughts, the door to the shop suddenly burst open with a loud bang. Marcus and Rufus, drenched in sweat and covered in flour, stormed in. Marcus's tunic was white with bread flour, while Rufus, smelling of wine, wore a garment nearly red with wine stains. Both, with the most exhausted yet angry expressions, glared at Severus.

"Severus!" Marcus shouted, waving his arms. "Baking bread? Who has ever done a job so hard? I work more than Romulus did building Rome!"

Rufus, hands on his hips, responded with a smirk: "You? Baking bread? I pour wine, calm angry customers, and keep glasses from breaking. You just touch flour, Marcus. I'm the one who truly works!"

"And you, Rufus," Marcus snapped back, "you drink wine all day and complain about work. May the gods bless you!"

"Silence, both of you," Severus interrupted, his face calm but inwardly laughing. "Why are you so tired? Does your master seem so harsh?"

"Harsh?" Rufus growled. "The master is worse than a rabid dog! Couldn't he at least pay me more?"

"And me too!" Marcus shouted. "The price of bread rises, but I still earn the same pay!"

Severus, leaning forward slightly and pretending to be serious, replied: "Alas, friends, your master does indeed seem difficult. But what if he were to ask you to work even harder?"

Marcus, now slightly panicked, exclaimed: "Work harder? Don't joke, Severus! I already work all day! The master is mad!"

Rufus manum ad caput levavit et addidit: "Quid faciemus? Num ad eum clamare debemus?"

Dum Severus de responsione iocosa cogitabat, ianua iterum aperta est, et Aurelia et Tullia, utraque ventrem gravidum ferentes, intraverunt. "Severe!" Aurelia clamavit. "Nos adiuvare debes! Lectos puerorum emere volumus, sed nescimus quid eligere."

Tullia, manibus in lateribus, vultu serio dixit: "Non possumus plus ambulare. Tu nobiscum venire debes, Severe. Tu solus consilium dare potes."

Severus, qui speraverat diem tranquillum habere, suspiravit. "Amicae carissimae," inquit, "nonne viri vestri hoc possunt? Marcus et Rufus quid agunt? Num nihil discunt?"

Aurelia, subridens, respondit: "Marcus solum panem videt. Rufus vinum amat. Non auxilium ab eis speramus."

Severus, manibus nummos colligens, surrexit et respondit: "Bene, bene. Venio. Sed mementote, amici, labores vestri non desinent!"

Dum Severus cum Aurelia et Tullia e taberna exibat, Marcus, qui ad mensam marmoream accesserat, manum ad patinam olivarum extendit. "Hic sumo unam," murmurat. "Nullus hoc observabit."

Rufus eum videns risit: "Marce, etiam cum famem habeas, fur es."

Severus, audiens verba, ad ianuam conversus subridens dixit: "Marce, caveas. Sunt multi oculi in hac taberna." Marcus, subito oliva fracta, manum retraxit, sed Rufus magno risu cachinnavit.

Severus, subridens, dum tabernam relinquit, sibilavit: "Mox omnes mirabimini. Sed, interim, laborate." Amici, ignari eius verborum significatus, inter se ridentes, cum sordidis vestibus et magna fatigatione tabernam reliquerunt, dum Severus consilia sua nova cogitabat. Finis capituli plenus spe et tumultu erat.

Rufus raised his hand to his head and added, "What should we do? Should we shout at him?"

While Severus was pondering a witty response, the door opened again, and Aurelia and Tullia, both heavily pregnant, entered. "Severus!" Aurelia exclaimed. "You must help us! We want to buy cribs for the babies, but we don't know what to choose."

Tullia, hands on her hips and with a serious expression, said, "We can't walk anymore. You must come with us, Severus. Only you can give us advice."

Severus, who had hoped for a peaceful day, sighed. "Dearest friends," he said, "can't your husbands handle this? What are Marcus and Rufus doing? Haven't they learned anything?"

Aurelia, smiling, replied, "Marcus only sees bread. Rufus loves wine. We can't expect help from them."

Severus, collecting the coins on the table, stood up and replied, "Fine, fine. I'll come. But remember, my friends, your work will not end!"

As Severus left the shop with Aurelia and Tullia, Marcus, who had approached the marble table, reached for a dish of olives. "I'll just take one," he muttered. "No one will notice."

Rufus, watching him, laughed. "Marcus, even when you're hungry, you're a thief."

Severus, overhearing their words, turned back toward the door and, smiling, said, "Marcus, beware. There are many eyes in this shop." Marcus, startled, dropped the olive he had just bitten into, but Rufus burst into roaring laughter.

Severus, grinning as he left the shop, whistled and said, "Soon, you will all be amazed. But in the meantime, keep working." The friends, oblivious to the meaning of his words, left the shop laughing, covered in flour and thoroughly exhausted.

Thus ended the chapter, full of hope and chaos, as Severus quietly contemplated his next plans while his companions carried on, caught between fatigue and hilarity.

Thesaurus Repertus

In horto prope villam, Aurelia et Tullia sub arbore magna sedebant, calore diei sub umbra se protegentes. Hortus floribus et herbis aromaticis plenus erat, sed utraque mulier vultu fessa videbatur. Aurelia manum super ventrem gravidum posuerat, dum Tullia calicem aquae lente hauriebat.

"Tullia," inquit Aurelia, subridens sed suspirans, "num cogitavisti quid futuri sint nostri liberi? Ego filium meum vidi in somnio togam albam gerentem, senatorem maximum Romae futurum."

Tullia risit et caput movit. "Senatorem? Tu semper magna somnias, Aurelia. Ego autem filiam volo. Fortasse divitem inveniat maritum, et melius vivamus."

Aurelia, subridens sed paulum provocans, respondit: "Non sinam filiam tuam vinum bibere cum Marci filio stulto! Num vis eam panem coquentem videre?"

Tullia oculos volvit et, ridens, respondit: "At ego tuam filiam in caupona mea laborare non sinam! Fortasse eam disces mittere ad naves onerarias. Melior labor est."

Dum mulieres ridebant, Marcus et Rufus, sudore et pulvere pleni, in hortum intraverunt. Marcus tunica farinosa indutus erat, dum Rufus vultu rubro, ex calore tabernae vinariae, advenit.

"Quid nunc est?" Marcus clamavit, se in scamnum iacens. "Mulier, panem coquere tam difficile est quam bellum gerere! Ego sum vir fortissimus, sed etiam Hercules defessus esset."

Aurelia, vultu irato, panem parvum de mensa cepit et in Marcum iecit. "Marce!" clamavit. "Tu solum farinam tangis, sed ego filium tuum portare debeo! Ne queraris."

Rufus, manibus caput terens, dixit: "Et ego tota die cum clientibus stultis litigo! Marce, tu farinam habes; ego autem vinum effundens soleo purgare."

A Treasure Discovered

In the garden near the villa, Aurelia and Tullia were sitting under a large tree, shielding themselves from the day's heat in the shade. The garden was full of flowers and aromatic herbs, but both women looked tired. Aurelia rested her hand on her pregnant belly, while Tullia slowly sipped a cup of water.

"Tullia," Aurelia said, smiling but sighing, "have you thought about what our children's futures will be? I saw my son in a dream wearing a white toga, destined to become a great senator in Rome."

Tullia laughed and shook her head. "A senator? You always dream big, Aurelia. I, on the other hand, want a daughter. Perhaps she'll marry a wealthy man, and we'll live better lives."

Aurelia, smiling but slightly teasing, replied, "I won't let your daughter drink wine with Marcus's foolish son! Do you want to see her baking bread all day?"

Tullia rolled her eyes and, laughing, retorted, "And I won't let your daughter work in my tavern! Perhaps you'll send her to help with cargo ships instead. That's a better job."

As the women laughed, Marcus and Rufus entered the garden, covered in sweat and dust. Marcus was wearing a flour-dusted tunic, while Rufus, red-faced from the heat of the wine shop, appeared exasperated.

"What now?" Marcus cried, throwing himself onto a bench. "Women, baking bread is as hard as waging war! I'm the strongest man, but even Hercules would be exhausted."

Aurelia, her face irritated, grabbed a small loaf of bread from the table and threw it at Marcus. "Marcus!" she shouted. "You only touch flour, but I have to carry your child! Stop complaining."

Rufus, rubbing his head with his hands, said, "And I spend my entire day arguing with foolish customers! Marcus, you deal with flour; I have to clean up spilled wine!"

Tullia manum levavit, vultu severo. "Vos duo estis ut pueri. Nos laboramus etiam, sed non tam clamorose."

Subito Severus, veste nitida et vultu composito, in hortum intravit. Manus ad caelum levans, voce gravi dixit: "Amici mei, satis querelarum! Hodie aliquid magni vobis monstrabo."

Marcus, vultu suspicaci, respondit: "Quid habes, Severe? Num vinum novum invenisti?"

Severus, subridens, caput movit. "Vinum? Non, Marce. Melius aliquid. Venite mecum ad tabernam meam. Hoc vestras fortunas mutabit."

Amici, paulum dubitantes sed curiosi, Severum ad tabernam secuti sunt. Severus eos in conclave posticum duxit, ubi terra paulum excavata videbatur. "Hic," inquit, "sub hoc loco aliquid magni latet. Marcus, da mihi manum."

Marcus, quamvis murmurans, pala cepit et terram removit. Subito arca vetus apparuit, clavis ad latus eius pendens. Rufus, vultu stupente, dixit: "Quid est hoc? Num thesaurum invenimus?"

"Videamus," Severus respondit, clavem arripiens et arcam aperiens. Intus nummi aurei et argentei lucidi et splendidi arcam replebant. Aurelia, manum ad os tenens, exclamavit: "Lucius! Hoc est aurum eius!"

Tullia, oculis coruscantibus, dixit: "Non possum credere! Divitiae iterum nostrae sunt."

Marcus, manibus avidis, unum nummum sustulit et risit. "Ecce, panem coquere non amplius necesse est!"

Severus, vultu placido sed subridente, tandem confessus est. "Amici mei, nunc aliquid confiteri debeo. Pistrinum et caupona ubi laboratis... mea sunt."

Rufus et Marcus, paene simul, clamaverunt: "Tua sunt? Severe, nos stultos fecisti!"

Tullia raised her hand with a stern expression. "You two are like children. We work too, but not as loudly as you."

Suddenly, Severus, dressed in neat clothes and with a composed demeanor, entered the garden. Raising his hands to the sky, he spoke in a serious tone: "My friends, enough with the complaints! Today I have something important to show you."

Marcus, with a suspicious look, replied, "What do you have, Severus? Have you discovered a new wine?"

Severus smiled and shook his head. "Wine? No, Marcus. Something better. Come with me to my shop. This will change your fortunes."

The friends, hesitant but curious, followed Severus to his shop. He led them to a back room, where the ground appeared partially dug up. "Here," he said, "beneath this spot lies something of great value. Marcus, lend me your hand."

Marcus, though grumbling, grabbed a shovel and started removing the earth. Suddenly, an old chest appeared, with a key hanging on its side. Rufus, his face filled with astonishment, said, "What is this? Have we found a treasure?"

"Let's find out," Severus replied, grabbing the key and opening the chest. Inside, bright and shiny gold and silver coins filled the chest. Aurelia, holding her hand to her mouth, exclaimed, "Lucius! This is his gold!"

Tullia, her eyes sparkling, said, "I can't believe it! The riches are ours again."

Marcus, with greedy hands, picked up one coin and laughed. "Look, baking bread is no longer necessary!"

Severus, his face calm but with a slight smile, finally confessed: "My friends, I have something to admit. The bakery and tavern where you work... they belong to me."

Rufus and Marcus, almost at the same time, shouted: "They're yours? Severus, you've made fools of us!"

Severus, manibus se defendens subridens, respondit: "Certe, sed mementote: melius est laborare quam otiosi esse. Videte, divitiae non semper felicitatem afferunt."

Aurelia et Tullia riserunt, dum Marcus et Rufus vultu incredulo Severum spectabant. "Severe," Marcus dixit, "ego tibi aliquid debitum reddam. Et panem tibi faciam quem numquam obliviscaris!"

Rufus, ridens, dixit: "Et ego vinum effundam super tunicam tuam."

Sed Severus, manibus apertis, clamavit: "Amici, ridete! Divitiae iterum nostrae sunt, et labor noster nos iunxit. Hoc est vinculum nostrum!"

Finis scaenae cum risu et clamore fuit, dum Severus in medio stabat, Marcus et Rufus irati sed subridens, et Aurelia et Tullia ex horto observabant, novas divitias suas cogitantes et amicitiam celebrantes.

Severus, raising his hands in mock defense while smiling, replied: "Certainly, but remember: it's better to work than to be idle. Look, wealth doesn't always bring happiness."

Aurelia and Tullia laughed, while Marcus and Rufus stared at Severus with incredulous expressions. "Severus," Marcus said, "I owe you something. And I'll bake you a loaf of bread you'll never forget!"

Rufus, laughing, added, "And I'll pour wine all over your tunic!"

But Severus, spreading his arms wide, exclaimed: "Friends, laugh! The riches are ours once again, and our labor has united us. This is our bond!"

The scene ended in laughter and shouts, with Severus standing at the center, Marcus and Rufus fuming but grinning, and Aurelia and Tullia watching from the garden, thinking about their newfound wealth and celebrating the friendship that tied them all together.

Felicitas et Concordia

Solis splendore aureo super Melitam, quinque amici in villa Marci et Aureliae congregati sunt ad convivium festive celebrandum. Atrium amplo lumine replebatur; mensa plena erat vinis, panibus calidis, et fructibus recentibus. Marcus, tunica mundiore quam umquam antea indutus, stolide circum spectabat, dum Aurelia flores mensae addidit.

"Haec mensa tam splendida est!" exclamavit Tullia, prope Aureliam sedens. "Quasi reginae et reges simus!"

"Reges?" Rufus, poculum vini in manu tenens, risit. "Si reges sumus, ego sum rex vini! Bibamus ad memoriam itineris nostri."

"Ad amicos, divitias, et... utinam nullos labores!" clamavit, poculum suum alte tollens. Omnes riserunt et pocula sua levaverunt.

Marcus, vinum lente sorbens, vultu serio addidit: "Nisi panem coquere sciam! Hoc certe iterum discere nolo. Panis et ego non amici sumus."

Aurelia, subridens sed oculis vibrantibus, respondit: "Panis coctus est, Marce, sed prope focum ardentem eris, si id iterum dicas." Omnes cachinnaverunt, dum Marcus manibus gesticulans quasi se defendebat.

Dum convivium crescendo gaudio pergebat, subito ianua crepuit, et nuntius ingressus est, pergamenum in manu tenens. Severus, qui semper tranquillus videbatur, surrexit et nuntium accepit. "Epistula?" quaesivit. "Quis misit?"

Severus, epistulam lente aperiens, vultu immutato legit. Subito risit et dixit: "A Lucio venit! Audite, amici. Scripsit se in provinciam remotam exsilio missum esse." Omnes brevi silentio perculsi sunt, donec Aurelia risum cohibere non potuit.

"Utinam semper sic maneat," Aurelia dixit, oculis micantibus. "Spero eum nunc in gelidis Britanniae paludibus ambulare. Bene ei conveniat cum glacie et barbaris."

Happiness and Harmony

Under the golden sunlight of Melita, the five friends gathered in Marcus and Aurelia's villa to celebrate a festive banquet. The atrium was filled with bright light; the table was laden with wines, warm bread, and fresh fruit. Marcus, wearing a cleaner tunic than ever before, stood proudly surveying the scene, while Aurelia added flowers to the table.

"This table is so splendid!" exclaimed Tullia, sitting beside Aurelia. "It's as if we were kings and queens!"

"Kings?" Rufus, holding a cup of wine in his hand, laughed. "If we're kings, then I'm the king of wine! Let us drink to the memory of our journey."

"To friends, wealth, and... hopefully, no more work!" he declared, raising his cup high. Everyone laughed and raised their cups in unison.

Marcus, sipping his wine slowly, added with a serious expression: "Unless it involves baking bread! That's one skill I certainly don't want to relearn. Bread and I are not friends."

Aurelia, smiling but with a sharp glint in her eyes, replied: "The bread may be baked, Marcus, but you'll find yourself near the fire if you say that again." Everyone burst into laughter as Marcus waved his hands dramatically, pretending to defend himself.

As the banquet grew livelier with joy, the door suddenly creaked, and a messenger entered, holding a scroll in his hand. Severus, who always appeared calm, rose and took the message. "A letter?" he asked. "Who sent it?"

Opening the letter slowly, Severus read it with an unchanged expression. Then, suddenly, he laughed and said, "It's from Lucius! Listen, friends. He writes that he's been exiled to a distant province."

For a moment, they all fell silent, stunned, until Aurelia could no longer hold back her laughter.

"Let's hope it stays that way," Aurelia said, her eyes sparkling. "I imagine him now trudging through the frozen swamps of Britannia. May he get along well with the ice and barbarians."

Tullia, ridens, addidit: "Britannia? Fortasse caput eius iam nive operitur. Nos nunc sine timore vivemus."

Marcus, vultu triumphantis, clamavit: "Haec est victoria! Num iterum me urina implebit? Non, amici mei, ego sum victor huius historiae!"

Dum omnes ridebant, Aurelia repente ventrem manu tenuit et suspiravit. "Amici, tempus est ut vos omnes audiatis. Tullia et ego aliquid magni dicere debemus."

Tullia, Aureliae manum tenens, subridens dixit: "Parvuli mox venient. Tempus est ut parentes fiatis."

Marcus et Rufus, paene simul, palluerunt. "Infantem lavare?" Marcus exclamavit, vultu terrore pleno. "Nihil peius scio! Num forte panem coquere iterum possum?"

"At ego," Rufus ridens sed anxius addidit, "vinulum infanti offeram! Num licet? Scilicet, vinum optimum."

Severus, spectans viros trepidantes, subridens dixit: "Nolite solliciti esse. Vos magnum laborem sustinere potestis. Sed nunc habeo meam confessionem: tabernas et cauponas vobis relinquere decrevi."

Rufus et Marcus subito clamaverunt: "Quid? Nos domini?"

"Ego, dominus pistrini?" Marcus exclamavit, manibus in capite positis. "Pessimum somnium est!"

Rufus, manibus in latera positis, respondit: "Caupona mea? Non potero sine vino vivere. Num taberna vinaria fiat etiam pistrinum?"

Severus, oculis subridentibus, manum levavit ut eos quietaret. "Amici, nolite timere. Ad Siciliam navigabo, ubi vinum bibam sine cura. Sed vobis confidentiam habeo. Labor vobis convenit."

Aurelia et Tullia ridebant, dum Marcus et Rufus inter se murmurabant. "Quid nunc faciemus?" Marcus sibilavit. "Melius est ut fuga consilium nostrum sit."

Tullia, laughing, added: "Britannia? Perhaps his head is already covered in snow. Now we can live without fear."

Marcus, with a triumphant expression, shouted: "This is victory! Will I be doused in urine again? No, my friends, I am the hero of this tale!"

As everyone laughed, Aurelia suddenly placed her hand on her belly and sighed. "Friends, it's time for you all to listen. Tullia and I have something important to announce."

Tullia, holding Aurelia's hand and smiling, said: "Little ones are on their way. It's time for you to become parents."

Marcus and Rufus, almost in unison, turned pale. "Wash a baby?" Marcus exclaimed, his face full of terror. "I can think of nothing worse! Perhaps I can go back to baking bread instead?"

"But I," Rufus added with a nervous laugh, "will offer the baby some wine! Surely, only the finest wine, of course."

Severus, watching the panicked men, smirked and said: "Don't worry. You've handled great challenges before. But now, I have my own confession: I've decided to leave the taverns and bakeries to you."

Rufus and Marcus shouted in surprise: "What? We're the owners now?"

"I, the master of a bakery?" Marcus exclaimed, placing his hands on his head. "This is a nightmare!"

Rufus, with his hands on his hips, replied: "And I'm to run a tavern? I can't survive without wine. Can we turn the tavern into a bakery instead?"

Severus, his eyes gleaming with amusement, raised his hand to calm them. "Friends, don't be afraid. I'm sailing to Sicily, where I'll drink wine without a care. But I trust you both. Work suits you."

Aurelia and Tullia laughed while Marcus and Rufus muttered to each other. "What are we going to do now?" Marcus whispered. "Fleeing might be the best plan."

"Non potestis fugere," Aurelia dixit, risu plena. "Vos estis patres futuri. Sustinete onus!"

Cum sol paulatim sub mare descenderet, quinque amici in porticum villae sedebant, manibus coniunctis, dum aurei radii diei finem notabant. Severus, spectans ad undas Siciliam versus, subridens dixit: "Forsitan Sicilia nos ad novum iter vocabit."

Marcus, poculum vini ad labra ferens, murmurat: "Utinam ibi panem coquere non debeam."

Omnes ridentes diem finiverunt, vitam suam chaoticam, plenam fortunae et stultitiae, sed etiam amicitia firmissima celebrantes.

"You cannot escape," Aurelia said, full of laughter. "You are soon-to-be fathers. Bear the responsibility!"

As the sun slowly sank into the sea, the five friends sat together on the villa's porch, their hands joined as the golden rays marked the day's end. Severus, gazing out toward the waves leading to Sicily, smiled and said, "Perhaps Sicily calls us to a new journey."

Marcus, raising a cup of wine to his lips, muttered, "I only hope I won't have to bake bread there."

Everyone laughed, ending the day by celebrating their chaotic lives—full of fortune and folly but also bound by the strongest friendship.

Vita Cotidiana in Carthagine Romana

1. Historia Carthaginis Romanae

Post Bellum Punicum Tertium, urbs Carthago, olim potentissima inter civitates Punicas, ab Romanis deleta est. Anno 146 a.C.n., exercitus Romanus urbem incensam diruit, civesque Carthaginienses servitute oppressit. Urbs tota in ruinas conversa est, et terra, ut Romani narrabant, sale aspersa est, ut nullum ibi iterum aedificium fieret. Sed post multos annos, Carthago iterum resurrexit, hoc tempore ut colonia Romana. Anno 44 a.C.n., Iulius Caesar urbem refecit eamque magnopere ampliavit.

Sub Imperio Romano, Carthago facta est urbs clara et dives. In ea vivebant mercatores, agricolae, et artifices, cum magna multitudine servorum. Forum Carthaginis, locus centralis, erat centrum negotiorum, ubi mercatores ex toto Imperio Romano veniebant ad merces vendendas et emendas. Hic locus semper plenus strepitu et tumultu erat, ubi nautae, negotiatores, et venditores conveniebant.

Carthago etiam thermas publicas et amphitheatra magnifica habuit. Inter haec, Thermae Antoninianae praeclarissimae erant, ubi cives lavari et otiari solebant. Amphitheatrum urbis quoque multis spectaculis gladiatoriis et venationibus inserviebat, et cives ex diversis classibus socialibus ibi conveniebant.

Templa quoque in Carthagine eximia erant. Templum Iunonis celeberrimum erat, quod montem urbis altissimum occupabat. In hoc templo Romani deos suos honorabant et caerimonias religiosas celebrabant. Hic locus sanctus non solum cultui religioso sed etiam conventibus politicis et socialibus aptus erat. Saepe magistratus Romani hic convenerunt ut de rebus publicis agerent.

Cultura Graeca et Romana simul in Carthagine vigebant, quod eam urbem variarum gentium et idearum reddidit. Romani linguam Latinam et Graecam hic adhibebant, sed etiam aliae linguae, sicut Punica, inter nonnullos adhuc in usu manebant. Haec mixtura culturam urbanam Carthaginis unicam fecit.

Daily Life in Roman Carthage

The History of Roman Carthage

After the Third Punic War, the city of Carthage, once the most powerful among the Punic states, was destroyed by the Romans. In 146 BCE, the Roman army burned the city to the ground, enslaved its Carthaginian inhabitants, and, according to Roman accounts, salted the earth so that no structures could ever rise again. However, after many years, Carthage rose again, this time as a Roman colony. In 44 BCE, Julius Caesar rebuilt and greatly expanded the city.

Under Roman rule, Carthage became a prosperous and illustrious city. Merchants, farmers, and artisans lived there, alongside a large population of slaves. The Forum of Carthage, the central square, was the hub of commerce, where merchants from all over the Roman Empire came to buy and sell goods. This area was always bustling with noise and activity as sailors, traders, and vendors gathered.

Carthage also boasted public baths and magnificent amphitheaters. Among these, the Antonine Baths were particularly famous, where citizens would go to bathe and relax. The city's amphitheater hosted many gladiatorial games and hunts, bringing together citizens from all social classes.

Carthage was also home to remarkable temples. The most renowned was the Temple of Juno, which occupied the city's highest hill. Here, Romans honored their gods and held religious ceremonies. This sacred site was not only for religious worship but also served as a venue for political and social meetings. Roman officials often convened here to discuss public matters.

Both Greek and Roman cultures flourished in Carthage, making it a melting pot of various peoples and ideas. Latin and Greek were the primary languages spoken, but other languages, such as Punic, were still used by some inhabitants. This cultural blend made the urban culture of Carthage unique.

Post saecula sub Romanis, Carthago tamen non semper pacem servavit. Anno 439 p.C.n., Vandalorum exercitus, duce Genserico, urbem oppugnavit et cepit. Vandali Carthaginem quasi novum regnum fecerunt et ecclesias multas deleverunt, dum multas divitias urbis sibi vindicarent.

Anno 533 p.C.n., imperator Byzantinus Iustinianus militibus suis, duce Belisario, urbem iterum cepit. Carthago sub Byzantinis restaurata est, sed numquam ad splendorem pristinum rediit.

Denique, anno 698 p.C.n., exercitus Arabum musulmanorum urbem expugnavit. Arabes Carthaginem deleverunt et multos incolas, qui musulmani fieri recusaverunt, in servitutem duxerunt. Post hanc vastationem, Carthago non amplius urbs magnifica fuit. Locus antiquus, qui olim caput Punicum et colonia Romana fuerat, paulatim in silentium et oblivionem descendit.

2. Insulae Romanae (Aedificia Popularia)

In Carthagine, sicut in aliis urbibus Romanis, multi cives in insulis, id est, aedificiis magnis et altis, habitabant. Insulae ex lapidibus aut lateribus exstructae erant et saepe quinque vel sex tabulata habebant. Inferiora tabulata divitibus locabantur, quia solidiora et tutiora erant. Superiora autem pauperibus destinabantur, quae instabilia et periculosa videbantur.

In insulis cubicula parva et angusta familiae tenebant. Locus saepe obscurus et plenus erat, sine fenestris aut spatiis ad aerem accipiendum. Multi cives in una cella vivebant, ubi etiam cibum parabant et dormiebant. Ignis saepe magnum periculum in insulis ferebat, quia tecta ex ligno incendia accendere solebant.

In urbe insulae magnae et compactae erant, sed ruri villae rusticae praevalebant. Villae maiores erant et pulchriorem vitam praebebant, cum hortis, fontibus, et aedificiis separatis ad servos. Sed villae rusticae plerumque divitum erant, qui agris magnis utebantur. Pauperes autem ruri in tuguriis habitabant, quibus saepe deerant tectum stabile et fenestrae.

After centuries under Roman rule, Carthage did not always enjoy peace. In 439 CE, the Vandal army, led by Genseric, attacked and captured the city. The Vandals established Carthage as the capital of their new kingdom, destroying many churches and seizing much of the city's wealth for themselves.

In 533 CE, the Byzantine Emperor Justinian sent his forces, led by General Belisarius, to reclaim the city. Carthage was restored under Byzantine rule, but it never regained its former splendor.

Finally, in 698 CE, an army of Muslim Arabs captured the city. The Arabs destroyed much of Carthage and enslaved many inhabitants who refused to convert to Islam. After this devastation, Carthage ceased to be a magnificent city. The ancient site, once the capital of the Punic world and a thriving Roman colony, gradually descended into silence and oblivion.

2. Roman Insulae (Apartment Buildings)

In Carthage, as in other Roman cities, many citizens lived in *insulae*, large and tall apartment buildings. These structures, made of stone or bricks, often had five or six stories. The lower floors were rented by wealthier inhabitants because they were sturdier and safer. The upper floors, however, were designated for poorer residents and were considered unstable and dangerous.

Families living in *insulae* occupied small and cramped rooms. These spaces were often dark, crowded, and lacked windows or proper ventilation. Many people lived in a single room where they cooked, ate, and slept. Fires were a constant threat in *insulae*, as wooden roofs and structures could easily ignite.

In the city, *insulae* were large and densely packed, while in the countryside, rustic villas were more common. Larger villas offered a more comfortable lifestyle, with gardens, fountains, and separate quarters for slaves. However, these rural villas were primarily owned by the wealthy, who managed vast estates. The poor in rural areas often lived in huts, which lacked stable roofs and windows.

3. Vita in Vico Urbano

Vita cotidiana in viis Carthaginis plena erat strepitu et tumultu. Forum et vici proximi semper turbis hominum referti erant: mercatores, venditores, servi, et liberi omnes simul movebant. Mercatus carnis, panis, piscium, et aliarum mercium cotidie clamores excitabat. Venditores clamabant: "Emite panem! Recentes pisces hic sunt!" Populus, pecuniam manu tenens, circum tabernas vagabatur, pretium mercimoniorum negotians.

Viae publicae Carthaginis saepe angustae erant, cum mulis et carris mercaturas vehentibus. Noxios odores stercoris et aquarum sordidarum vici urbis implebant. Sed non deerant aspectus iucundi: musici canebant, ioculatores saltabant, et artifices suas res vendebant.

Servi maximi momenti in vita urbana fuerunt. In foro panem coquebant, amphoras portabant, aut vestimenta purgabant. Servi nonnumquam mercedem accipiebant, ut tandem libertatem adipiscerentur. Liberti, olim servi, plerumque negotia urbana gerebant, ut vinum venderent aut vestes suterent. Liberti saepe gratias dominis suis agebant, qui eos liberaverant.

Quamquam tumultus et chaos cotidiani urbem implebant, Carthago tamen urbs viva et operosa erat. Eius cives vitam diversam agebant, ab opulentis mercatoribus ad humiles servos. Sed omnes una communitatem faciebant, quae Carthaginem Romanam clarissimam et memorabilem reddebat.

4. Fullonica Romana

In civitatibus Romanis, fullonicae, id est officinae coriariorum, magnae partes in vita cotidiana agebant. Processus coriarius erat ars laboriosa sed necessaria ad societatem Romanam, quia coria ad tunicas militares, calceos, et alias res fabricandas utebantur.

3. Life in the Urban Quarter

Everyday life in the streets of Carthage was full of noise and commotion. The forum and its nearby districts were always bustling with crowds of people: merchants, vendors, slaves, and children all moved together in a chaotic dance. Markets for meat, bread, fish, and other goods were alive with shouting. Vendors cried out, "Buy bread! Fresh fish here!" as people, holding their coins, wandered among the stalls, haggling over prices.

The public streets of Carthage were often narrow, crowded with mules and carts transporting goods. The air was filled with unpleasant odors from dung and dirty water flowing through the streets. However, there were also pleasant sights: musicians played, acrobats danced, and artisans displayed their crafts for sale.

Slaves played an essential role in urban life. In the forum, they baked bread, carried amphoras, or washed clothing. Occasionally, slaves earned wages, which they could save to eventually buy their freedom. Freedmen, who were former slaves, often ran urban businesses, selling wine or tailoring clothes. Freedmen frequently expressed gratitude to their former masters who had granted them freedom.

Despite the daily turmoil and chaos, Carthage was a lively and industrious city. Its inhabitants led diverse lives, from wealthy merchants to humble slaves. Yet, together they formed a community that made Roman Carthage one of the most vibrant and memorable cities of the ancient world.

4. The Roman Fullonica

In Roman cities, *fullonicae*, or tanneries, played a significant role in everyday life. The tanning process was a labor-intensive but essential craft for Roman society, as leather was used to make military tunics, shoes, and other goods.

Primum, coria ex animalibus detracta in aquis sordidis macerabantur, ut pilis et carne purgarentur. Postea in lacus cum lotio humano immergebantur. Lotio, quod naturalem ammoniacum continebat, corium molliebatur et purgabat. Servi vel operarii coria pedibus calcabant, processu difficili et taetro, quia odor lotii saepe intolerabilis erat.

Postquam coria mollia fiebant, coloribus tingebantur vel oleis unguebantur ad flexibilitatem augendam. Fullones, qui hunc laborem exercebant, saepe in vicis sordidissimis urbis habitabant, quia officinae suae odores foetidos fundebant. Propter naturam laboris sui, fullones statum sociale humilem habebant. Tamen munus eorum oeconomiae urbis maxime necessarium erat.

5. Pistrinum Romanum

Panis erat cibus principalis Romanorum. Pistrina, id est officinae panis, in omnibus civitatibus inveniebantur. Processus panem faciendi cum molendinis incipiebat. Grana in molis lapideis frangebantur, ubi servi aut asini molas circumducebant. Farina inde obtenta in massas aquae et salis commiscebatur.

Postquam massa formata est, panis in furnis magnis coquebatur. Furni rotundi, lateribus exstructi, calorem diu retinebant. Panes formae varias habebant: rotundi, quadrati, vel etiam ornati pro diebus festis. Panis vulgaris plebi durus et spissus erat, sed divites panem molliorem, cum melle aut lacte mixtum, praeferebant.

Pistrinae saepe partes domorum aut tabernarum occupabant. Nonnumquam familiae nobiles proprias officinas in domibus suis habebant. Sed pistrinae publicae, ubi panis venalis coquebatur, maximae erant et urbem universam pane praebebant.

First, hides removed from animals were soaked in dirty water to be cleansed of hair and flesh. Then they were immersed in vats of human urine. The urine, containing natural ammonia, softened and cleaned the leather. Slaves or workers would tread on the hides with their feet, a laborious and unpleasant process, as the smell of urine was often unbearable.

After the hides were softened, they were dyed with colors or treated with oils to increase their flexibility. The *fullones*, or leatherworkers, who carried out this work, often lived in the dirtiest parts of the city because their workshops emitted foul odors. Due to the nature of their work, *fullones* had low social status. Nevertheless, their role was crucial to the economy of the city.

5. The Roman Bakery

Bread was the staple food of the Romans. *Pistrinae*, or bakeries, were found in every Roman city. The bread-making process began with mills. Grain was ground in stone mills operated by slaves or donkeys, which turned the heavy millstones. The resulting flour was mixed with water and salt to create dough.

After the dough was shaped, it was baked in large ovens. These round ovens, constructed from stone, retained heat for long periods. Bread came in various shapes: round, square, or even decorated for festive occasions. Common bread for the masses was hard and coarse, while the wealthy preferred softer bread, often mixed with honey or milk.

Bakeries were often located in parts of houses or shops. Sometimes noble families had private bakeries within their homes. However, public bakeries, where bread was made for sale, were the largest and supplied the entire city with bread.

6. Cauponae Romanae

Cauponae, id est tabernae ubi cibus et potio veneunt, erant loca vivida sed interdum male famae. In cauponis viatores et cives urbis congrediebantur, ubi vinum bibebant et cibos simplices edebant. Panis, olea, caseus, et oliviae inter cibos communiter offerebantur. Vina, quae diluta aqua bibebantur, tam vilia quam pretiosa inveniri poterant.

Cauponae saepe ad angulos viarum vel prope fora positae erant. Plurimae cauponae in tabernis inferioribus insularum inveniebantur, cum parvis mensis et scamnis. Atmosphaera ibi tumultuosa erat: voces altas, risus, et interdum rixas audire poteras. Propter frequentiam ebrietatis et lites, cauponae famam infamem habebant.

Sed cauponae etiam partes sociales et commerciales implebant. Negotiatores ibi conventus habebant, et nautae portus ibi remanebant. Caupones, id est domini cauponarum, interdum fraudis accusabantur, quia vinum falsificatum vendere vel pretia augere solebant. Nihilominus, cauponae erant partes integrales vitae urbanae Romanae.

7. Mercatores in Orbe Romano

Mercatores in mundo Romano, sicut Severus, fundamentum oeconomiae erant. Negotiatores per mare aut terram iter faciebant, merces inter urbes imperii permutantes. Carthago et Melita portus clari erant, ubi mercatores vinum, oleum, triticum, et alia mercimonia importabant et exportabant.

Vinum ex Italia, oleum ex Hispania, et triticum ex Aegypto Carthaginem saepe veniebant. Inde mercatores haec bona per Africam, Siciliam, et alios portus disseminabant. Melita, propter situm maritimum suum, locus magni momenti erat, ubi mercatorum naves transibant. Mel ibi praecipue notum erat, simul cum cera ad totum Imperium exportata.

6. Roman Taverns

Cauponae, or taverns where food and drink were sold, were lively but sometimes ill-reputed places. In these establishments, travelers and city dwellers gathered to drink wine and eat simple meals. Bread, oil, cheese, and olives were commonly served. Wines, diluted with water, ranged from cheap to expensive varieties.

Taverns were often located at street corners or near forums. Most taverns were found on the ground floors of apartment buildings (*insulae*), furnished with small tables and benches. The atmosphere was noisy: one could hear loud voices, laughter, and occasionally fights. Because of frequent drunkenness and disputes, taverns often carried a bad reputation.

Nevertheless, *cauponae* played important social and commercial roles. Merchants held meetings there, and sailors from the port often stayed in the taverns. The tavern keepers (*caupones*), however, were sometimes accused of fraud, as they were known to sell watered-down wine or inflate prices. Despite this, *cauponae* were an integral part of Roman urban life.

7. Merchants in the Roman World

Merchants in the Roman world, like Severus, were the backbone of the economy. These traders traveled by sea or land, exchanging goods between cities of the empire. Carthage and Melita were prominent ports where merchants imported and exported wine, oil, grain, and other goods.

Wine from Italy, oil from Spain, and grain from Egypt frequently arrived in Carthage. From there, merchants distributed these goods across Africa, Sicily, and other ports. Melita, due to its maritime location, was a significant hub where merchant ships passed through. Honey, for which Melita was especially known, along with wax, was exported throughout the Empire.

Mercatores, licet divites fieri possent, saepe magna pericula sustinebant. Tempestates maritimae, piratae, et mercimonia perdita eos semper minabantur. Sed propter diligentiam et industriam suam, mercatores vitam Romanam ditaverunt, urbium et provinciarum commercium amplificantes.

8. Mulierum Munus in Societate Romana

In societate Romana, mulieres, sicut Aurelia et Tullia, vitam plenam laboris et officiorum gerebant. Quamquam potestas publica plerumque virorum erat, mulieres tamen fundamentum familiae et vitae domesticae constituebant.

Mulieres in matrimonium saepe adulescentes dabantur, et munus earum principale erat familiae curam gerere et liberos procreare. Uxor bonum exemplum castitatis et diligentiae praebere debebat. Aurelia et Tullia, mulieres nobiles, non solum pro familiis suis laborabant, sed etiam saepe in hortis flores colebant aut vestes texebant.

Vita cotidiana mulierum domum maxime circumscribebatur, sed mulieres divitiores interdum thermas aut fora visitabant. Etiam convivia interdum participabant, ubi honorem domus ostendebant. Mulieres pauperiores, autem, saepe in tabernis laborabant vel merces vendebant, ut familiae suae vitam sustentaret.

In familia, mulieres etiam pro gravidarum curis et liberorum educatione respondebant. Maternitas erat virtus maxima, et mulieres ut matres laudabantur. Tullia, exempli gratia, iam cogitabat de nomine filiae suae et spe eius futuri mariti divitis.

Merchants, although they could become wealthy, often faced great risks. Maritime storms, pirates, and lost cargo constantly threatened them. However, through their diligence and industry, merchants enriched Roman life, expanding trade between cities and provinces.

8. The Role of Women in Roman Society

In Roman society, women, like Aurelia and Tullia, led lives full of labor and responsibilities. Although public power was mostly held by men, women nonetheless formed the foundation of family and domestic life.

Women were often married as adolescents, and their primary role was to care for the household and raise children. A wife was expected to set a good example of chastity and diligence. Aurelia and Tullia, noblewomen, not only worked for their families but also cultivated flowers in gardens or wove textiles.

Daily life for women was largely confined to the home, but wealthier women occasionally visited baths or forums. They sometimes participated in banquets, where they demonstrated the honor of the household. Poorer women, however, often worked in shops or sold goods to sustain their families.

Within the family, women were also responsible for caring for pregnant relatives and educating children. Motherhood was considered the highest virtue, and women were praised as mothers. Tullia, for example, was already thinking about a name for her daughter and dreaming of her marrying a wealthy man in the future.

9. Partus et Infantes in Antiqua Roma

Partus erat eventus magni momenti in vita mulierum Romanarum. Quando mulier gravida erat, familia tota de salute matris et infantis sperabat. Parandae erant res necessariae: lintea ad infantem involvendum et lectus parvus ad dormiendum. Mulieres praegnantes saepe auxilia matronarum aut obstetricum petebant.

Cum partus inciperet, obstetrices domum veniebant ut mulieri adessent. Partus non sine periculis erat, sed mulieres pro fortitudine sua laudabantur. Postquam infans natus est, parentes eum purgabant et linteo involvebant. Si infans in familia acceptus erat, pater eum sollevabat et in gremio suo collocabat.

Die octavo (pro puellis) aut die nono (pro pueris) post nativitatem, dies lustricus celebrabatur. Hoc die infanti nomen dabatur, et caerimonia purificationis peragebatur. Infans munera accipiebat, sicut armillas aut ludos, et tota familia de eius futuro cogitabat. Dies lustricus initium vitae infanti legitimae signabat.

Parentes Romani infantes diligebant, sed etiam severi erant. Pueri a tenera aetate disciplinam et pietatem discere debebant. Aurelia, filium suum futurum iam sibi imaginabatur togam albam in foro gerentem, dum Tullia de filia sua in convivio nobilium cogitabat.

---

10. Servi et Libertini

Servi in societate Romana vitam arduam et plenam laboris gerebant. In urbe, servi in variis officiis laborabant: quidam in domibus divitum coquebant, vestimenta purgabant, vel liberos curabant. Alii autem in negotiis publicis aut mercatoriis occupabantur, sicut servi Severi, qui amphoras in portu portabant.

Servi in familiae vita essentiales erant. Dominus bonos servos saepe laudabat et aliquando benigne tractabat, sed multi servi vitam asperam sub duris dominis agebant. Servi tamen spe manumissionis vivebant. Si servus fideliter laboraret, dominus ei libertatem concedere poterat.

9. Childbirth and Infants in Ancient Rome

Childbirth was a significant event in the lives of Roman women. When a woman was pregnant, the entire family hoped for the health of both mother and child. Necessary items were prepared: linens to swaddle the baby and a small crib for sleeping. Pregnant women often sought the assistance of matrons or midwives.

When labor began, midwives would come to the home to assist the woman. Childbirth was not without risks, but women were praised for their endurance. After the baby was born, the parents would clean and swaddle the infant in a linen cloth. If the baby was accepted into the family, the father would lift the child and place it on his lap, symbolizing his acknowledgment.

On the eighth day (for girls) or the ninth day (for boys) after birth, the *dies lustricus* (naming day) was celebrated. On this day, the child was given a name, and a purification ceremony was performed. The infant received gifts, such as bracelets or toys, and the family contemplated the child's future. The *dies lustricus* marked the beginning of the infant's legitimate life.

Roman parents loved their children but were also strict. From a young age, children were taught discipline and piety. Aurelia already imagined her future son wearing a white toga in the forum, while Tullia dreamed of her daughter attending a banquet of nobles.

10. Slaves and Freedmen

Slaves in Roman society led arduous lives filled with labor. In the city, slaves worked in a variety of roles: some cooked, cleaned clothes, or cared for children in wealthy households. Others were engaged in public or commercial tasks, such as the slaves of Severus, who carried amphoras in the port.

Slaves were essential to family life. A master often praised loyal slaves and occasionally treated them kindly, but many slaves lived harsh lives under strict masters. Despite this, slaves lived with the hope of manumission. If a slave worked faithfully, their master might grant them freedom.

Libertini, id est servi manumissi, libertatem obtinuerant sed adhuc aliqua officia erga dominos suos exsolvere debebant. Multi libertini in negotiis successerunt et pecuniam suam coacervaverunt. Exemplo sunt libertini qui tabernas vinarias aut cauponas in urbe rexerunt. Etiam libertini aliquando filios suos ad magistratus aut ordines altos promovere potuerunt.

Servi et libertini fundamentum vitae urbanae Romanae formaverunt. Quamquam servi statum humilem habebant, multi spe meliorem vitam habere vivebant, et libertini saepe pontem inter classes sociales constituebant. Severus, libertinus dives, exemplum huius successus ostendit, dum mercatores ex variis partibus Imperii in tabernam suam venire videbat.

11. Nummi Romani: Aurum et Argentum

In Imperio Romano, nummi varias formas et valores habebant. Tres materiae principales ad nummos fabricandos adhibebantur: aurum, argentum, et aes (id est, aeramentum). Nummi aurei, qui solidissimi erant, summum valorem habebant. Aureus, ex auro purissimo factus, saepe ad magnas pecunias solvendas adhibebatur, sicut in mercaturis internationalibus aut muneribus divitum.

Nummi argentei, sicut denarius, frequentissimi in vita cotidiana erant. Denarius saepe ad cibum, vestimenta, aut alia necessaria in foro emenda utebatur. Plebis et mercatorum praecipuus usus fuit. Ad minoras transactiones, nummi aerei, sicut sestertius vel as, adhibebantur. Hi nummi viliores erant, sed in negotiis simplicibus, ut panis aut olei emptione, valde utiles.

Nummi in tota urbe et provinciis circulabant. Mercatores nummos ex uno loco ad alium ferebant, dum in portubus, sicut in Carthagine, denarii pro vinis, oleis, et tritico permutabantur. Tabernarii, caupones, et fabri omnes nummos accipiebant. Servi saepe mercedem parvam in nummis accipiebant, quam servabant aut domino suo tradebant.

Freedmen (*libertini*), who were formerly enslaved, had gained their freedom but often still owed certain duties to their former masters. Many freedmen found success in business and amassed wealth. For instance, freedmen often managed wine shops or taverns in urban areas. Occasionally, freedmen could even advance their children to higher magistracies or prominent social ranks.

Slaves and freedmen together formed the backbone of urban Roman life. Although slaves held a low social status, many lived with the hope of achieving a better life, and freedmen often served as a bridge between social classes. Severus, a wealthy freedman, exemplified this success as he welcomed merchants from across the Empire into his thriving shop.

11. Roman Coins: Gold and Silver

In the Roman Empire, coins came in various forms and values. Three primary materials were used for minting coins: gold, silver, and bronze (*aes*). Gold coins, the most valuable, were used for significant transactions. The *aureus*, made from pure gold, was often employed in international trade or as gifts among the wealthy.

Silver coins, such as the *denarius*, were the most commonly used in daily life. The *denarius* was often spent on food, clothing, or other essentials at the market and was the main currency for the common people and merchants. For smaller transactions, bronze coins like the *sestertius* or the *as* were used. These coins had lower value but were indispensable for everyday purchases like bread or oil.

Coins circulated widely throughout cities and provinces. Merchants carried them from one location to another, and in ports like Carthage, *denarii* were exchanged for wine, oil, and grain. Shopkeepers, tavern owners, and craftsmen all accepted coins. Even slaves occasionally received small wages in coins, which they saved or handed over to their masters.

Vera fides nummorum a civibus et mercatoribus postulabatur. Nummi corrupti, id est, minus auri vel argenti continentes, interdum in mercatibus inveniebantur. Hoc fraus magna erat, et magistratus Romani leges duras contra falsarios imposuerunt. Nihilominus, nummi Romani fundamentum stabilitatis oeconomicae Imperii formaverunt.

12. Tributum et Corruptio in Provinciis Romanis

Tributum, id est vectigalia et onera pecuniaria, magna pars administrationis Romanae erat. Cives Romani et provinciales, sicut in Carthagine, tributa solvere debebant. Tributa ex variis formis constabant: census (tributum fundorum), portorium (tributum mercaturae), et capitarium (tributum personae).

In provincia Carthaginiensi, agricolae triticum suum ad granaria publica saepe dare cogebantur. Mercatores autem portoria in portubus solvebant, cum merces suas importabant aut exportabant. Haec vectigalia ad aerarium Romanum mittebantur, sed etiam ad magistratus locales, qui provincias regebant.

Corruptio autem in provinciae administratione frequens erat. Publicani, id est collectores vectigalium, saepe plura exigebant quam lex permittebat. Illi, qui pecuniam dare recusabant, interdum minas aut poenas acerbas patiebantur. Magistratus Romani in provinciis divitias sibi saepe accumulabant, potestate sua abutentes. Exempla huius avaritiae saepe in litteris Romanis invenimus, sicut in orationibus Ciceronis contra Verrem, qui in Sicilia multos spoliavit.

Provinciales, sicut agricolae et mercatores in Carthagine, saepe ob onera tributi laborabant. Sed aliqui, sicut Severus, ex mercaturis suis lucrum fecerunt, non obstante tributo. Pecuniae publicae, quamvis aliquando male gestae, etiam vias, thermas, et alia publica aedificia provinciis praestiterunt.

True value in coins was demanded by citizens and merchants alike. Corrupted coins—those containing less gold or silver than claimed— were sometimes found in markets. This was considered a major fraud, and Roman magistrates imposed harsh penalties on counterfeiters. Nevertheless, Roman coins served as the foundation of the Empire's economic stability.

12. Taxation and Corruption in the Roman Provinces

Taxes (*tributum*), which included levies and financial contributions, formed a major part of Roman administration. Both Roman citizens and provincials, such as those in Carthage, were required to pay taxes. Taxes came in various forms: *census* (land tax), *portorium* (trade tax), and *capitarium* (poll tax).

In the province of Carthage, farmers were often compelled to deliver their wheat to public granaries. Merchants paid *portoria* at the ports when importing or exporting goods. These revenues were sent to the Roman treasury but also funded local magistrates who governed the provinces.

Corruption, however, was widespread in provincial administration. *Publicani* (tax collectors) often demanded more than what was legally permitted. Those who refused to pay could face threats or severe punishments. Roman magistrates in the provinces frequently amassed great wealth, abusing their power. Examples of such greed are frequently found in Roman literature, such as Cicero's speeches against Verres, who plundered many in Sicily.

Provincials, such as farmers and merchants in Carthage, often struggled under the burden of taxes. However, some, like Severus, managed to profit from their trade despite the taxation. Public funds, though sometimes mismanaged, also contributed to the construction of roads, baths, and other public buildings within the provinces.

13. Navigatio Maritima Romana

Romani mare nostrum, quod Mediterraneum vocamus, magnum et periculosum iter saepe faciebant. Navigatio maritima fundamentum commercii et communicationis inter provincias Imperii Romani erat. Naves Romanae, variis generibus, tam ad merces transportandas quam ad milites vehendos utebantur.

Naves onerariae, quae gravia onera portabant, latas carinas et alta latera habebant, ut fluctibus altis resisterent. Triremes, quae in bellis adhibebantur, tres ordines remorum habebant et celeritatem praestabant. In navibus onerariis, merces mercatorum, sicut vinum, oleum, triticum, et amphorae, in carina diligenter ordinabantur. Nautae Romani cursum rectum tenere solebant, stellis nocturnis et vento utentes. Portus maiores, ut Ostia, Carthago, et Alexandria, semper nautis et mercatoribus patuerunt.

Iter per mare nostrum, tamen, saepe periculis completum erat. Tempestates subito oriebantur, ventis violentis fluctibusque altis naves impellentibus. Nautae, cum tempestas appropinquabat, vela contrahere et ancoras iacere solebant, sed non semper tempestates evitari poterant. Multi nautae, cum mercibus suis, in mari perierunt.

Praeterea, piratae saepe periculum nautis attulerunt, praesertim in regione Ciliciae. Piratae naves onerarias oppugnabant et merces rapiebant. Romani tandem Pompeium Magnum miserunt, qui mare nostrum a piratis purgavit. Post eius victoriam, navigatio securior facta est.

Navigatio maritima, quamvis periculosa, necessaria erat. Sine ea, Imperium Romanum magnas divitias et merces—vinum ex Italia, triticum ex Aegypto, oleum ex Hispania—non habuisset. Nautae et mercatores, quamvis pericula magna subierint, vitam maritimam Romanam florere fecerunt.

13. Roman Maritime Navigation

The Romans often traversed the vast and dangerous *Mare Nostrum* (the Mediterranean), which served as the foundation for commerce and communication between the provinces of the Roman Empire. Roman ships of various types were used for transporting goods as well as troops.

Cargo ships (*naves onerariae*), designed to carry heavy loads, had wide hulls and high sides to withstand rough waves. Warships like *triremes*, used in military campaigns, featured three rows of oars and were known for their speed. On cargo ships, merchants' goods, such as wine, oil, grain, and amphorae, were carefully stowed in the hold. Roman sailors navigated with precision, relying on the stars at night and the wind during the day. Major ports like Ostia, Carthage, and Alexandria were always bustling with sailors and merchants.

However, journeys across the *Mare Nostrum* were fraught with danger. Sudden storms often arose, bringing violent winds and towering waves. When a storm loomed, sailors would furl the sails and drop anchor, but these measures did not always ensure safety. Many sailors, along with their cargo, were lost to the sea.

In addition to natural hazards, pirates posed a significant threat, particularly in the region of Cilicia. These pirates attacked cargo ships and stole valuable goods. Eventually, the Romans dispatched Pompey the Great to eliminate the pirate menace. After his victory, maritime travel became much safer.

Despite the risks, maritime navigation was indispensable. Without it, the Roman Empire would not have enjoyed its vast wealth and access to essential goods such as Italian wine, Egyptian grain, and Spanish oil. Sailors and merchants, though they faced immense dangers, made Roman maritime life thrive.

14. Melita in Temporibus Romanis

Melita, quae hodie Malta vocatur, parva insula in medio mari Mediterraneo sita, magnae significationis fuit in temporibus Romanis. Haec insula punctum transitus essentiale erat in itineribus maritimis inter Africam, Siciliam, et Italiam. Melita tam in commerciis quam in rebus militaribus Romanorum locum habuit.

Melita propter mel, quod apes ibi conficiebant, praeclarissima erat. Hoc mel tam dulce et purum erat ut in toto Imperio quaereretur. Praeterea, insula textilibus notissima erat. Lana et linum ibi confecta in urbes magnas, sicut Roma et Carthago, exportabantur. Vestimenta ex Melita saepe luxuriae signum habebant et apud divites Romanos valde desiderabantur.

Portus Melitae, quamvis parvus, naves Romanas suscipiebat. Nautae et mercatores ibi aquam, cibum, et instrumenta navalia comparabant. Melita etiam locus reficiendarum navium erat, quia insula lignum ad naves fabricandas idoneum praebebat. Multae naves ibi reparatae sunt antequam iter longum per mare nostrum continuarent.

Vita in Melita composita erat ex agricolis, mercatoribus, et nautis. Agricolae mel et oleum produxerunt, dum mercatores illa bona exportabant. Praeterea, milites Romani in insula locati erant ut piratas longe tenerent et commercium tutarentur.

Cultura Melitae vestigia Graeca et Punica servavit. Ante adventum Romanorum, insulam Carthaginienses tenebant. Cum Romani insulam ceperunt, culturam Graecam et Punicam cum suis moribus coniunxerunt. Templa, thermae, et fora in insula aedificata sunt, et Melita pars plena Imperii Romani facta est.

In summa, Melita, quamvis insula parva, in commerciis Romanis magnum pondus habuit. Apium mel, textilia, et refectio navium eam locum clarum in Imperio Romano reddiderunt. Vita cotidiana ibi tam laboriosa erat quam in magnis urbibus Romanis, sed semper cum unda maris et ventis Mediterraneis circumdatis.

14. Melita in Roman Times

Melita, known today as Malta, was a small island located in the middle of the Mediterranean Sea and of great significance during Roman times. This island was an essential transit point for maritime journeys between Africa, Sicily, and Italy. Melita played an important role in both Roman commerce and military operations.

Melita was most famous for its honey, produced by the bees on the island. This honey was so sweet and pure that it was highly sought after throughout the Roman Empire. Additionally, the island was renowned for its textiles. Wool and linen produced in Melita were exported to major cities such as Rome and Carthage. Clothing made from Melitan textiles was often seen as a symbol of luxury and highly desired by wealthy Romans.

The port of Melita, though small, welcomed Roman ships. Sailors and merchants stopped there to resupply with water, food, and naval equipment. Melita also served as a ship repair hub, as the island provided suitable timber for shipbuilding. Many vessels were repaired there before continuing their long voyages across the *Mare Nostrum.*

Life in Melita consisted of farmers, merchants, and sailors. Farmers produced honey and olive oil, while merchants exported these goods. In addition, Roman soldiers were stationed on the island to deter pirates and protect trade routes.

The culture of Melita retained traces of Greek and Punic influence. Before the arrival of the Romans, the island was controlled by the Carthaginians. When the Romans conquered it, they blended Greek and Punic traditions with their own customs. Temples, baths, and marketplaces were built on the island, integrating it fully into the Roman Empire.

In summary, although Melita was a small island, it held great importance in Roman trade. Its honey, textiles, and ship repair facilities made it a key location in the Roman Empire. Daily life on Melita was as industrious as in larger Roman cities, but always surrounded by the waves and winds of the Mediterranean Sea.

15. Iustitia Romana et Scelesti

In Imperio Romano, iustitia et disciplina magni momenti erant ad ordinem publicum servandum. Lex Romana clara et firma erat, poenas gravissimas in eos qui eam violabant imponens. Malefactores, sicut Lucius et socii eius, saepe in foro vel in basilica iudicabantur. Praetores, magistratus responsabiles pro iudiciis, causas audiebant et sententias dabant.

Si quis furti convictus esset, poena ei imposita dependebat ex magnitudine furti. Fur minor plerumque pecuniam aut bonum restituebat, sed fur maior, qui res pretiosas vel divitias auferebat, saepe in servitutem damnabatur. Si vero homicidium aut scelus grave commiserat, damnatus capitis supplicium subibat. Poenae includebant crucifixionem pro servis aut decollationem pro civibus Romanis, quae considerabatur poena mitior.

Aliqui scelesti ad amphitheatra mittebantur, ubi cum bestiis in arena pugnare cogebantur. Hoc spectaculum saepe ad plebem delectandam fiebat, sed etiam monere omnes de gravitate legum Romanarum volebat. Malefactores pauperes duris poenis multabantur, sed divites interdum veniam emere poterant, quia pecunia magnum valorem in iudiciis habebat.

Cohortes urbanae, id est milites in urbe Romana constituti, ordinem publicum custodiebant. Hi milites, sub praefecto urbi, scelestos comprehendebant et tumultus sedabant. In Carthagine et aliis urbibus maioribus, similes custodes publici erant. Cohortes urbanae in foro et vicis frequenter deambulabant, ne furta aut seditiones fierent. Praeterea, vigilias nocturnas faciebant, ut incendia et caedes in urbe impedirent.

Romani leges suas tam severas quam iustas existimabant. Lex non solum scelestos puniebat, sed etiam omnes cives Romanos a periculis protegebat. Si leges violatae essent, civitas ipsa periclitabatur, et id Romani nullo modo tolerabant.

15. Roman Justice and Criminals

In the Roman Empire, justice and discipline were of great importance for maintaining public order. Roman law was clear and strict, imposing severe punishments on those who violated it. Criminals, such as Lucius and his associates, were often judged in the forum or basilica. Praetors, the magistrates responsible for legal proceedings, would hear cases and deliver sentences.

If someone was convicted of theft, the punishment depended on the severity of the crime. A minor thief usually had to return the stolen goods or pay compensation, but a major thief, who stole valuable items or large amounts of wealth, was often condemned to servitude. If a person committed murder or a serious crime, they were sentenced to capital punishment. Penalties included crucifixion for slaves or decapitation for Roman citizens, the latter being considered a more lenient punishment.

Some criminals were sent to amphitheatres, where they were forced to fight wild animals in the arena. This spectacle was often organized to entertain the populace but also served as a stark warning about the seriousness of Roman laws. Poor offenders were harshly punished, while the wealthy could sometimes buy their way out of trouble, as money held significant influence in legal proceedings.

The *cohortes urbanae*, urban military units stationed in the city of Rome, were responsible for maintaining public order. These soldiers, under the command of the *praefectus urbi*, apprehended criminals and suppressed riots. In Carthage and other major cities, similar public guards existed. The *cohortes urbanae* frequently patrolled the forum and streets to prevent thefts and uprisings. They also conducted nighttime watches to prevent fires and murders within the city.

The Romans regarded their laws as both severe and fair. The law not only punished wrongdoers but also protected all Roman citizens from harm. Violating the laws endangered the very fabric of the state, something the Romans were determined not to tolerate.

16. Exilium in Mundo Romano

Exilium, id est relegatio vel expulsio hominum a civitate, erat poena communis in Imperio Romano. Exilium saepe in eos qui contra rem publicam peccaverant aut scelera magna commiserant, ut Lucius, imponebatur. Exilium, quamvis poena mitior quam mors videretur, tamen gravis fuit, quia homines patria et familia privabantur.

Exules ad loca remota mittebantur, saepe ad insulas aut provincias longinquas, ubi nec Romam nec amicos suos videre poterant. Exilium saepe duobus modis fiebat: relegatio et deportatio. Relegatio mitior erat, quia exules bona sua retinere poterant, sed deportatio severior, quia omnia bona exulibus auferebantur. Lucius, si deportatus esset, in locum asperum et desertum, ut Britanniam aut insulam parvam, missus esset.

Historia Romanorum multos exules praeclaros commemorat. Cicero, clarus orator, olim a senatu relegatus est, quia leges contra populum violasse putabatur. Postea tamen, populus eum restituit, et Cicero ad gloriam suam reversus est. Alia exempla includunt Ovidium, poetam qui propter carmina sua Augustus imperator in exilium ad Pontum misit. In exilio, Ovidius epistulas tristissimas scripsit, quibus desiderium patriae et familiae suorum expressit.

Exilium interdum in provincias solitudinis plenissimas trahebat. Britannia, quae frigida et pluviosa erat, saepe exules recepit. Alii in insulas parvas, sicut Pandateriam vel Delum, mittebantur, ubi cibo et aqua parci debebant. Exules tamen, si fortuna eos faveret, interdum veniam impetrare poterant et ad patriam redire.

Romani exilium non solum ut poenam, sed etiam ut modum disciplinae civium viderunt. Homines, qui contra ordinem et leges peccaverant, exemplo aliis fiebant. Exules in perpetuo timore erant, scientes se semper sub oculis imperatoris aut senatus manere.

16. Exile in the Roman World

Exile, or *relegatio* and *deportatio*, was a common punishment in the Roman Empire. It was often imposed on individuals who had committed crimes against the state or serious offenses, such as Lucius. Although exile was considered a milder punishment than death, it was still severe, as it deprived individuals of their homeland and family.

Exiles were sent to distant locations, often to islands or far-flung provinces where they could neither see Rome nor contact their friends. Exile typically came in two forms: *relegatio* and *deportatio*. *Relegatio* was less severe, as exiles were allowed to retain their property, while *deportatio* was harsher, stripping individuals of all their possessions. If Lucius were deported, he might have been sent to a harsh and desolate place like Britannia or a small, isolated island.

Roman history remembers many notable exiles. Cicero, the famous orator, was once relegated by the Senate because he was accused of violating laws against the people. However, the populace later restored him, and Cicero returned to his former glory. Another example is the poet Ovid, who was exiled by Emperor Augustus to Tomis (on the Black Sea) due to his controversial writings. In exile, Ovid penned sorrowful letters expressing his longing for his homeland and loved ones.

Exile often led to places of profound solitude. Britannia, known for its cold and rainy climate, frequently received exiles. Others were sent to small islands like Pandateria (modern Ventotene) or Delos, where food and water were scarce. However, with fortune and determination, some exiles managed to obtain pardons and return to their homeland.

The Romans saw exile not only as a punishment but also as a tool for disciplining citizens. Those who violated order and laws served as examples to others. Exiles lived in constant fear, knowing they remained under the watchful eyes of the emperor or Senate. In this way, exile became a symbol of both the authority of Roman law and the consequences of defiance.

In fine, exilium erat modus puniendi qui terribilem separationem ab urbe et familia inferebat, sed etiam Romanis indicium clarum dabat de potestate legum et disciplinae in Imperio Romano. Lucius et alii scelesti, si exules facti essent, non solum poenam gravem subierunt, sed etiam vitam solitariam et miseram sustinere debuerunt.

17. De Re Coquinaria Romana et Conviviis

Cibus et convivium apud Romanos magni momenti erant, non solum ad famem satiandam, sed etiam ad gaudium et amicitias colendas. Marcus et Aurelia, si convivium splendidum parare vellent, multa genera ciborum suis amicis offerrent.

In cena Romana tres partes principales erant: gustatio, prima mensa, et secunda mensa. Gustatio, quae initium cenae erat, saepe includebat ova, olivas, et caseum. Marcus, qui panem et mel semper amabat, hos cibos pro convivis parare curabat. Prima mensa, id est pars principalis cenae, carnem et pisces continere poterat. Porcus assus, pullus, vel murena in mensa apponebantur. Aurelia porcum herbis et speciebus condiebat, dum Marcus vinum diluebat.

Cibaria plebeiorum simplicia erant. Panis, oleum, et puls, id est farina aqua cocta, in mensis plebis saepe apparabantur. Divites tamen, sicut Marcus et Aurelia, etiam delicias habebant, sicut ostreas, lucustas, et garum, liquamen piscis celeberrimum. Haec omnia ex regionibus Imperii Romani ad urbes vehebantur: triticum ex Aegypto, vinum ex Italia, et oleum ex Hispania importabantur.

Secunda mensa, id est dulcia, saepe fructus recentes vel siccos habebat. Mala, pira, fici, et uvae in mensa ponebantur. Divites etiam placentas cum melle et nucibus edebant. Marcus et Rufus saepe vinum optimum petebant ut convivium suum decoraretur. Vinum Romanum autem numquam purum bibebatur, sed semper aqua, melle, vel herbis dulcorabatur.

Exile was a method of punishment that inflicted a terrible separation from one's city and family, but it also served as a clear indication to the Romans of the power of laws and discipline within the Roman Empire. Lucius and other criminals, if they became exiles, not only endured severe punishment but also had to sustain a solitary and miserable life.

17. Roman Cuisine and Banquets

Food and banquets were of great importance to the Romans, not only to satisfy hunger but also to cultivate joy and friendships. Marcus and Aurelia, if they wanted to prepare a splendid banquet, would offer many kinds of food to their friends.

In a Roman dinner, there were three main courses: the appetizer (*gustatio*), the main course (*prima mensa*), and dessert (*secunda mensa*). The appetizer, which marked the beginning of the meal, often included eggs, olives, and cheese. Marcus, who always loved bread and honey, made sure to prepare these foods for his guests. The main course, or the centerpiece of the meal, could consist of meat and fish. Roast pork, chicken, or moray eel would be served. Aurelia would season the pork with herbs and spices, while Marcus diluted the wine.

The food of common people (*plebeians*) was simple. Bread, olive oil, and *puls* (a porridge made of flour and water) were often found on their tables. However, the wealthy, like Marcus and Aurelia, enjoyed delicacies such as oysters, lobsters, and *garum*—the famous fish sauce. All these goods were transported to the cities from different regions of the Roman Empire: wheat from Egypt, wine from Italy, and olive oil from Spain.

The dessert (*secunda mensa*), or sweets, often consisted of fresh or dried fruits. Apples, pears, figs, and grapes were placed on the table. The wealthy also enjoyed cakes with honey and nuts. Marcus and Rufus often sought the finest wine to elevate their banquet. Roman wine, however, was never drunk pure but was always sweetened with water, honey, or herbs.

Roman banquets, with their luxurious spreads and convivial atmosphere, were a cornerstone of social life, symbolizing not only abundance but also the deep connections among friends and families.

Convivia non solum ad comedendum, sed etiam ad colloquia et lusus habebantur. Post cenam hospites saepe cantabant, ludos aleae ludebant, vel carmina recitabant. Marcus, qui semper iocos amabat, convivas saepe risu implebat. Aurelia autem, gravitate moderata, musicos vel poetas invitabat ut convivium suum augeret.

Romani cibum et vinum non solum pro utilitate, sed etiam pro voluptate aestimabant. Marcus et Aurelia, sicut alii Romani, in conviviis laetitiam et societatem inveniebant.

18. De Ludo et Otiis Romanis

Otium et ludus magna pars vitae Romanae erant. Romani, cum laboribus exonerarentur, varia genera voluptatis quaerebant. Marcus, Aurelia, Rufus, et Severus saepe ad spectaculum vel ludum conveniebant ut tempus suum liberum fruerentur.

Unum ex maximis spectaculis Romanis erat theatrum. In theatris, comoediae et tragoediae ab actoribus Romanis vel Graecis perferebantur. Comoediae Plauti et Terentii valde amabantur. Marcus, cum Severus theatrum frequentaret, saepe de iocis comoediarum ridebat, dum Aurelia et Tullia tragoedias graviores praeferrebant.

Aliud spectaculum populi erant munera gladiatoria. Gladiatores, in amphitheatris pugnantes, magnas turbas ad se trahebant. Spectatores, Marcus incluso, suos gladiatores praeferrebant et clamores altissimos emittebant ut eos sustinerent. Severus autem, qui pugnas saepe nimis cruentas esse putabat, haec spectacula raro frequentabat.

Circenses, id est cursus quadrigarum, in Circo Maximo vel aliis locis publicis magnopere amabatur. Equi celerissimi et aurigae audacissimi pro victoria certabant. Rufus semper factionem viridem favebat, dum Marcus factionem albam praetulit. Clamor et tumultus circum implebant, dum aurigae quadrigas suas per spatia volabant. Multi Romani etiam pecuniam in factionibus collocabant, spe lucri.

Banquets were not only for eating but also for conversation and games. After dinner, guests often sang, played dice games, or recited poetry. Marcus, who always loved jokes, frequently filled the guests with laughter. Aurelia, on the other hand, with her moderate demeanor, would invite musicians or poets to enhance the elegance of the banquet.

Romans valued food and wine not only for their practicality but also for their pleasure. Marcus and Aurelia, like other Romans, found joy and camaraderie in their banquets.

18. Games and Leisure in Roman Life

Leisure and play were an important part of Roman life. When free from their labors, Romans sought various forms of entertainment. Marcus, Aurelia, Rufus, and Severus often gathered at shows or games to enjoy their free time.

One of the most prominent forms of entertainment was the theater. In theaters, comedies and tragedies were performed by Roman or Greek actors. The comedies of Plautus and Terence were especially popular. Marcus, attending the theater with Severus, often laughed at the jokes in the comedies, while Aurelia and Tullia preferred the weightier tragedies.

Another popular spectacle was gladiatorial games. Gladiators, fighting in amphitheaters, drew massive crowds. Spectators, including Marcus, cheered for their favorite gladiators, shouting loudly to support them. Severus, however, who often found the fights too brutal, rarely attended these events.

Chariot races (*circenses*), held in the Circus Maximus or other public arenas, were also widely loved. The fastest horses and the boldest charioteers competed for victory. Rufus always supported the green faction, while Marcus favored the white faction. Cheers and commotion filled the arena as charioteers raced their quadrigae (four-horse chariots) across the tracks. Many Romans even placed bets on the factions, hoping for a profit.

Plebeii saepe ludos simpliciores habebant. In tabernis aut cauponis, alea et tesserae ludebantur. Rufus et Marcus interdum vinum bibentes et ludos aleae iocose disputantes inveniebantur. Tullia et Aurelia in hortis vel thermis otium suum agebant, ubi cum aliis matronis colloquebantur.

Thermae, publicae balneae, locus maximus ad relaxandum et colloquendum erant. Romani ibi lavabant, ungebantur, et cum amicis de variis rebus loquebantur. Severus saepe thermas visitabat, non solum ut corpus purgaret, sed etiam ut novas mercaturas cum aliis locupletibus viris tractaret.

Otium apud Romanos non significabat inertiam, sed occasionem ad corpus et animum recreandum. Marcus, Aurelia, et amici eorum, sicut ceteri Romani, inter spectacula et otium vitam suam laeti replebant. Sive in theatro, sive in circo, sive in tabernis, ludus et laetitia vitam Romanam vividam reddebant.

19. De Humore Romano

Apud Romanos, humor magna pars vitae cotidianae erat. Romani, ut animum recrearent et societatem laetitia imbuerent, iocis et fabulis comicis valde gaudebant. Ioca non solum in tabernis et conviviis narrabantur, sed etiam in comoediis et satiris scripta erant, quae totum populum delectabant.

Comoedia Romana, praesertim opera Plauti et Terentii, exemplum optimum humoris Romani praebet. Plautus fabulas scribebat, quae servos callidos, dominos stultos, et amatores miseros ostendebant. Spectatores de erroribus et stultitia personarum ridebant. Exemplum clarum est servus, qui dolis et astutia dominum superat. Hic modus comicus saepe etiam in *Friends in Carthage* apparet, ubi Marcus et Rufus in rebus comicis saepe stulti vel absurdi fiunt.

The plebeians often enjoyed simpler games. In taverns or inns, dice and board games were played. Rufus and Marcus were sometimes found drinking wine and playfully arguing over dice games. Tullia and Aurelia spent their leisure time in gardens or bathhouses, where they conversed with other matrons.

The baths, public bathing places, were prime locations for relaxation and socializing. Romans would bathe, be anointed with oils, and talk with friends about various matters. Severus often visited the baths, not only to cleanse his body but also to negotiate new trade deals with other wealthy men.

Leisure for Romans did not mean idleness but an opportunity to refresh both body and mind. Marcus, Aurelia, and their friends, like other Romans, filled their lives with joy between spectacles and leisure. Whether in the theater, the circus, or taverns, games and merriment made Roman life vibrant.

19. On Roman Humor

For the Romans, humor was an essential part of daily life. To lift their spirits and bring joy to their social interactions, they greatly enjoyed jokes and comic stories. Jokes were told not only in taverns and banquets but were also written into comedies and satires that delighted the entire population.

Roman comedy, particularly the works of Plautus and Terence, offers an excellent example of Roman humor. Plautus wrote plays that featured clever slaves, foolish masters, and miserable lovers. Spectators laughed at the mistakes and foolishness of the characters. A clear example is the clever slave who outwits his master through tricks and cunning. This comedic style often appears in *Friends in Carthage*, where Marcus and Rufus frequently find themselves in comical or absurd situations.

Satira, genus litterarium distinctum apud Romanos, quoque humor gravem et criticum coniungebat. Scriptores, sicut Iuvenalis et Horatius, mores hominum et vitia civitatis in lucem ponebant. Per satiram Romani superbiam divitum, avaritiam mercatorum, et stultitiam plebis ridere solebant. Licet satira severa videretur, tamen populus eam utilem habebat, quia societatem meliorem facere posse credebatur.

In vita cotidiana, Romani inter se iocis utebantur. Tabernae saepe loca risus et iocositatis erant. Venditores in foro, dum merces suas laudabant, interdum clientes deridebant. Servi quoque dominis suis, licet caute, subridebant, sicut in Plautinis comoediis videmus.

Marcus et Rufus, sicut comici Romani, saepe risum inter amicos provocant. Rufus de labore suo in caupona queritur, dum Marcus de pistrino ridet. Similiter, scaenae in quibus Severus amicos suos dolis utitur, ad Plautinam traditionem comicam appropinquant.

Humor apud Romanos erat et delectatio et instrumentum ad mores hominum corrigendos. Sive in comoediis, sive in conviviis, sive in satira, risus Romanorum non solum ad voluptatem, sed etiam ad instructionem valebat.

20. De Ordinibus Socialibus et Tensionibus

Imperium Romanum magna diversitate ordinum socialium regebatur. Divites, mercatores, plebeii, et servi omnes in una societate vivebant, sed saepe magnae inter eos tensiones exsistebant. Haec diversitas etiam in fabula *Friends in Carthage* apparet, ubi amici ex diversis vitae partibus oriuntur et cum Lucio, qui potentiam suam male utitur, conflictus habent.

Divites et Nobiles: Divites Romani, sicut Lucius, domos magnas habebant et luxuriosam vitam agebant. Hi homines saepe vi et pecunia ad imperium suum conservandum utebantur. Lucius exemplum typicum est huius ordinis, qui inferiores saepe opprimebat. Nobiles quoque in convivis splendidis congregabantur, ubi vinum optimum bibebant et de re publica vel mercatibus disputabant.

Satire, a distinct literary genre among the Romans, combined humor with serious critique. Writers like Juvenal and Horace highlighted the flaws of individuals and the vices of society. Through satire, Romans mocked the pride of the wealthy, the greed of merchants, and the foolishness of the common people. Although satire could appear harsh, the public valued it as a tool for improving society.

In everyday life, Romans often used jokes with one another. Taverns were frequent places of laughter and humor. Merchants in the forum, while praising their goods, sometimes mocked their customers. Servants also occasionally made sly jokes about their masters, though cautiously, as seen in Plautine comedies.

Marcus and Rufus, like Roman comic characters, often provoked laughter among their friends. Rufus complained about his work in the tavern, while Marcus made jokes about the bakery. Similarly, scenes in which Severus tricks his friends reflect the Plautine comic tradition.

Humor among the Romans was both a source of entertainment and a tool for moral correction. Whether in comedies, banquets, or satires, Roman laughter served not only for pleasure but also for instruction.

20. On Social Classes and Tensions

The Roman Empire was governed by a society of great social diversity. The wealthy, merchants, plebeians, and slaves all lived within one system, but significant tensions often existed among them. This diversity is also evident in *Friends in Carthage*, where friends come from different walks of life and face conflicts with Lucius, who abuses his power.

The Wealthy and the Nobles: Wealthy Romans, like Lucius, lived in grand houses and led luxurious lives. These individuals often relied on force and wealth to maintain their power. Lucius is a typical example of this class, which frequently oppressed those below them. Nobles also gathered at splendid banquets, where they drank the finest wines and discussed politics or trade.

Mercatores: Mercatores, sicut Severus, inter divites et plebeios medios erant. Quamquam pecuniam saepe magna industria sibi comparabant, tamen non semper a divitibus honorabantur. Severus exemplum est mercatoris callidi, qui amicos suos interdum adiuvat, interdum autem dolis in eos utitur. Mercatores etiam pericula sustinebant, sicut tempestates maritimas vel piratas, sed eis vita mobilis et divitiae praemia erant.

Plebeii: Plebs urbana, sicut Marcus et Rufus, vitam simplicem et difficilem agebat. Hi homines in pistrinis, cauponis, et foris laborabant, saepe multis horis sine magno mercede. Marcus, qui in pistrino panem coquit, et Rufus, qui in caupona vinum fundere debet, exempla sunt plebeiorum qui laboribus suis societatem sustentabant. Plebeii tamen saepe divites deridebant, praesertim cum luxuria eorum nimia videretur.

Servi et Libertini: Servi infima ordinis pars erant, saepe sine libertate aut dignitate. Servi panem coquebant, coria tingebant, aut tabernas purgabant. Aliqui tamen libertatem adipisci poterant et liberi facti liberti appellabantur. Liberti saepe negotia gerebant et etiam divites fieri potuerunt, sed semper vestigia servitutis portabant.

Tensiones inter hos ordines saepe erant. Divites plebeios despiciebant, dum plebeii divites avaritia accusabant. Servi dominis suis invidebant, sed liberti, cum divites fierent, saepe superioritatem erga plebem ostendebant. In *Friends in Carthage,* hae tensiones per relationes inter amicos et Lucium clare apparent. Amici, qui ex plebe et mercatura oriuntur, contra Lucium, qui potentiam suam abutit, consurgunt.

In fine, societas Romana, quamvis ordines et distinctiones rigidas haberet, tamen omnes in una urbe vel provincia iungebat. Marcus, Rufus, Severus, Aurelia, et Tullia exempla sunt quomodo diversi ordines possint amicitia et communi labore iungi, etiamsi tensiones inter eos exstent. Fabula haec, sicut societas ipsa, ostendit vitam Romanam plenam esse conflictuum, sed etiam occasionum ad reconciliationem et amicitiam.

Merchants: Merchants, like Severus, were positioned between the wealthy and the plebeians. Although they often acquired wealth through significant effort, they were not always respected by the elite. Severus exemplifies the clever merchant, who sometimes helps his friends but also uses tricks against them. Merchants faced risks such as maritime storms and pirates, but the rewards of a mobile lifestyle and riches compensated for these dangers.

Plebeians: The urban plebeians, like Marcus and Rufus, led simple and difficult lives. These people worked in bakeries, taverns, and markets, often for long hours and little pay. Marcus, who bakes bread in the bakery, and Rufus, who pours wine in the tavern, are examples of plebeians whose labor sustained society. However, plebeians often mocked the wealthy, especially when their luxury appeared excessive.

Slaves and Freedmen: Slaves were the lowest class, often living without freedom or dignity. They baked bread, dyed leather, or cleaned shops. However, some could achieve freedom and were called freedmen. Freedmen often managed businesses and could even become wealthy, but they always bore the marks of their former servitude.

Tensions often existed among these classes. The wealthy despised the plebeians, while the plebeians accused the rich of greed. Slaves envied their masters, but freedmen, once they became wealthy, often displayed a sense of superiority over the common people. In *Friends in Carthage*, these tensions are clearly reflected in the relationships between the friends and Lucius. The friends, originating from the plebeian and mercantile classes, rise against Lucius, who abuses his power.

In the end, Roman society, despite its rigid hierarchies and distinctions, united everyone within the same city or province. Marcus, Rufus, Severus, Aurelia, and Tullia exemplify how different classes could bond through friendship and shared labor, even when tensions arose among them. This story, like Roman society itself, demonstrates that life in Rome was full of conflicts, but also opportunities for reconciliation and friendship.

21. De Vestibus et Ornatu Romanorum

Romani, tam viri quam feminae, vestes suas non solum ad corpus tegendum, sed etiam ad statum suum ostendendum utebantur. Vestis erat signum dignitatis, classis socialis, et occasionis.

Vestes Virorum:

Viri Romani togas et tunicas gerere solebant. Tunica, vestis interior, ex lana aut lino conficiebatur et simplicior erat. Omnes cives Romani tunicas gerebant, sed togae solum civibus Romanis licebat. Toga alba, quae *toga pura* aut *virilis* appellabatur, signum dignitatis erat. Magistratus aut senatores togam praetextam, cum purpureo limbo, induebant, ut auctoritatem suam ostenderent.

Vestes Feminarum:

Feminae Romanae stolas et pallas gerebant. Stola, quae erat vestis longa et ampla, solum matronis licebat. Palla, vestis exterior, super stola vel tunica circumvolutabatur et saepe coloribus variis ornabatur. Feminae etiam fibulis et gemmis ornamenta suas vestes decorabant.

Status in Vestibus:

Status socialis clare in vestibus Romanis apparebat. Divites vestes ex lana delicata vel serico conficiebant, dum pauperes vestes simplices ex materia rudi gerebant. Colores quoque signum status erant: purpura, quae ex conchyliis rara conficiebatur, pretiosa erat et solum divitibus licebat.

Vestes Romanae non solum corporis tegumenta erant, sed etiam imago dignitatis et status, quae in foro et conviviis clare ostendebatur.

21. On the Clothing and Adornment of the Romans

The Romans, both men and women, used their clothing not only to cover their bodies but also to display their status. Clothing was a symbol of dignity, social class, and occasion.

Men's Clothing:

Roman men typically wore togas and tunics. The tunic, an inner garment, was made of wool or linen and was simpler in design. All Roman citizens wore tunics, but togas were reserved exclusively for Roman citizens. The white toga, known as the *toga pura* or *toga virilis*, was a symbol of dignity. Magistrates or senators wore the *toga praetexta*, adorned with a purple border, to signify their authority.

Women's Clothing:

Roman women wore *stolas* and *pallas*. The *stola*, a long and flowing garment, was reserved for matrons. The *palla*, an outer garment, was draped over the *stola* or tunic and often came in various colors. Women also adorned their clothing with brooches and gemstones for decoration.

Status in Clothing:

Social status was clearly reflected in Roman attire. The wealthy wore garments made from fine wool or silk, while the poor wore simple clothing made from coarse materials. Colors also indicated status: purple, which was made from rare shellfish dye, was expensive and permitted only for the wealthy.

Roman clothing was not merely a means of covering the body but also a representation of dignity and status, clearly displayed in the forum and at banquets.

22. De Usu Lotii in Vita Romana

Urina, quamvis hodie vilis videatur, apud Romanos usus multiplicis habebat et in multis partibus vitae cotidianae adhibebatur.

In Fullonicis:

In officinis fullonicis, ubi vestes lavabantur et tingebantur, urina magnum usum habebat. Lotio, quae naturalem ammiacum continebat, vestes purgabat et coria molliebat. Operarii pedibus vestes calcabant in lotio, ut sordes tollerentur et textilia purificarentur. Quamvis odor lotii molestus esset, tamen fullones sine hoc liquore opus suum perficere non poterant.

In Medicina:

Romani etiam urina in medicina utebantur. Ciceronis temporibus, urina interdum ad vulnera lavanda aut infectiones curandas adhibebatur. Credere solebant lotium certis morbis remedio esse.

In Tributis:

Urina tantae utilitatis erat ut imperator Vespasianus tributa super lotium imposuerit. Cloacae publicae et latrinae urinam collegerunt, quae deinde fullonicis aut aliis officinis vendebatur.

Romani, qui omnia ad usum aptare sciebant, etiam lotium humilem in rem magni momenti convertebant. Ex hoc dicto, *"Pecunia non olet,"* ortum habet, quod ad Vespasianum refertur.

22. On the Use of Urine in Roman Life

Urine, though considered insignificant today, had multiple uses in Roman society and was applied in many aspects of daily life.

In Fullonicae (Laundry Workshops):

In fullonicae, workshops where clothes were washed and dyed, urine played a crucial role. The ammonia contained in urine was used to cleanse clothes and soften leather. Workers would tread on the garments in urine to remove dirt and purify textiles. Although the smell of urine was unpleasant, fullers could not complete their tasks without this liquid.

In Medicine:

Romans also used urine in medicine. In Cicero's time, urine was occasionally applied to wash wounds or treat infections. It was believed that urine had curative properties for certain ailments.

In Taxes:

Urine was so valuable that Emperor Vespasian imposed taxes on it. Public sewers and latrines collected urine, which was then sold to fullers or other workshops.

The Romans, known for their resourcefulness, turned even humble urine into something of great importance. From this practice, the phrase *"Pecunia non olet"* ("Money doesn't stink") originated, attributed to Vespasian.

23. De Canibus in Societate Romana

Canes magnum locum in vita Romanorum habebant, tam in domibus quam in viis urbanis. Hi animalia utilissima, sed interdum molestissima, erant.

Canes Domestici:

In domibus divitum, canes saepe tamquam custodes et amici familiares habebantur. Famosi erant canes Molossi, qui fortes et fideles erant. Canes parviores quoque matronis placebant, ut eos domi vel in hortis tenerent.

Canes Custodes et Molesti:

In viis urbanis, canes vagabundi saepe apparebant. Hi canes, qui cibum ex tabernis aut mercatis quaerebant, interdum venditores vexabant. Aliquando in rixis inter se mordebant, tumultumque in plateis excitabant. Scaenae cum canibus, sicut illa in *Friends in Carthage*, saepe comica erant, sed etiam imaginem vitae tumultuosae urbanae praebebant.

Romani canes amabant et utilitatem eorum agnoscebant, sed etiam eos iocis in litteris et picturis deridebant.

---

24. De Mercatibus et Foro Romano

Forum Romanum erat centrum vitae urbanae, ubi mercatura, politica, et vita socialis in unum conveniebant.

Structura Mercati:

In foro, tabernae et bancae in ordine positae erant. Mercatores merces suas in mensis vel tabulis ponebant, ut populus eas inspiceret et emeret. Loca venditae saepe specifica erant: carnis taberna, piscis taberna, et panis taberna. Praeterea, ambulantes venditores per vias clamabant, merces suas laudantes.

23. On Dogs in Roman Society

Dogs held an important place in Roman life, both in homes and in the urban streets. These animals were highly useful but sometimes quite troublesome.

Domestic Dogs:

In the homes of the wealthy, dogs were often kept as both guardians and loyal companions. Famous among them were Molossian dogs, known for their strength and loyalty. Smaller dogs were also popular among matrons, who enjoyed keeping them at home or in their gardens.

Guard Dogs and Stray Dogs:

In urban streets, stray dogs often appeared. These dogs, scavenging food from shops or markets, occasionally annoyed vendors. Sometimes they fought among themselves, causing commotion in the streets. Scenes involving dogs, like those in *Friends in Carthage*, were often comedic but also depicted the chaotic aspects of urban life.

The Romans appreciated dogs and their usefulness but also humorously mocked them in literature and art.

24. On Markets and the Roman Forum

The Roman Forum was the center of urban life, where commerce, politics, and social activities converged.

Structure of the Market:

In the forum, shops and stalls were arranged in an orderly fashion. Merchants displayed their goods on tables or stands for people to inspect and buy. Specific areas were designated for different goods: a butcher's shop, a fishmonger's shop, and a baker's shop. Moreover, street vendors roamed the streets, loudly praising their wares.

Negotium et Pretium:

Negotiatio pars maxima mercatus erat. Romani pretium pro mercibus saepe negotiabantur. Venditores clamabant: *"Panis recentissimus! Olivae optimissimae!"* Populus, pecuniam manu tenens, mercibus pretium minuebat.

Variatio Mercimoniorum:

Merces ex totis partibus Imperii Romani in foro inveniebantur. Triticum ex Aegypto, vinum ex Italia, oleum ex Hispania, et textilia ex Melita ad urbes vehebantur. Mercatus erat locus ubi culturae et bona diversarum gentium conveniebant.

Forum Romanum non solum locus mercaturae, sed etiam centrum vitae communis erat, ubi cives et peregrini conveniebant, ut vitam vibrantem et plenam experirentur. Marcus et Severus saepe in foro ad merces spectandas et pretium negotiandum inveniebantur, imaginem vivam vitae Romanae ostendentes.

Negotiation and Price:

Negotiation was a key part of the market. Romans frequently bargained over the price of goods. Vendors would shout: "Freshest bread! Finest olives!" People, holding their money in hand, would haggle to lower the price of goods.

Variety of Goods:

Goods from all parts of the Roman Empire could be found in the market. Wheat from Egypt, wine from Italy, olive oil from Spain, and textiles from Melita were transported to the cities. The market was a place where cultures and goods from diverse regions converged.

The Roman Forum was not only a place of commerce but also a hub of communal life, where citizens and foreigners gathered to experience a vibrant and lively atmosphere. Marcus and Severus were often found in the forum inspecting goods and bargaining prices, offering a vivid glimpse into Roman life.

www.discoverlatin.com

Find more Latin books and other resources at

www.discoverlatin.com